THE COMPLEAT KLEZMER

HENRY SAPOZNIK

with
Pete Sokolow

Tara Publications, Cedarhurst, N.Y.

DISTRIBUTED BY

HAL•LEONARD®
CORPORATION

7777 W. BLUEMOUND RD. P.O. BOX 13819 MILWAUKEE, WI 53213

ISBN 0-933676-10-7

PRINTED IN THE UNITED STATES

CONTENTS

A DANK*

This book was a long time in coming and I want to thank the people
who helped make it happen:

Pete Sokolow my partner in a plethora of cultural undertakings, champion
transcriber, colleague and pal.
Lynn Dion, my editor, for tirelessly offering perceptive perspective, and a
24 hour emergency editing service beyond the call of duty.
Velvel Pasternak prolific publisher with the patience of a dozen Jobs.
Judy Helfand for helping locate some of the photos used here.
Harry Bolick for cover design. and David Ryan, cover photo-retoucher
Dan Peck, my "Apple source".
Richard Spottswood, ethnic discographer extraordinaire.
Michael Schlesinger of Global Village Music.
My parents Pearl and Zindel Sapoznik.
Wendy Marcus, the original klezmette.
The YIVO Institute for Jewish Research and its Max and Frieda Weinstein
Archives of Sound Recordings and Photo Archives for its unique collections
of primary, secondary and tertiary materials related to this and other Yiddish subjects.
Most of all I'd like to thank the klezmer musicians and their descendents who
helped me immeasurably: Dave Tarras, Joe Helfenbein, Leon Schwartz, the late
Louis Grupp, Doris Kandel, Edward Elenkrig, and Sid Beckerman. It is to them,
and to those who continue their music, that this book is dedicated.

*Thanks loads

I

I remember my bar mitzvah.

My parents had hired one of the top New York City klezmer clarinetists to play at the reception. So there he was on the bandstand blowing some of the best bulgars in the business and all I wanted to do was to crawl into the nearest, deepest hole

"Can't this guy play anything modern?", the bar mitzvah kvetsched.

Up to that point all my life had been spent in the presence of this kind of music. I made no distinction between the Hasidic nigunim we sang on the schoolbus going to Lubavitch yeshiva and the klezmer and Yiddish music ubiquitously heard at the Catskill hotels where we sang during Peysekh. I thought everybody had a cantor father who wandered around the house softly humming the High Holiday liturgy to himself. It was all the same to me.

And I wanted to have done with it.

I actually just wanted to be a normal kid (Beaver Cleaver would do) who didn't go to yeshiva, sing in a choir, or have to shlep to the mountains every spring.

He was playing klezmer music and I wanted rock'n'roll.

But something's changed.

In the last decade, klezmer music, this traditional instrumental music of the Jews of Eastern Europe, has attracted a robust reinterest in the American Jewish community. From Sheepshead Bay to Seattle new klezmer musicians are appearing and older ones reappearing. Growing audiences across the country are are made up of older folks who are reminded of their younger days, and younger folks for whom these will someday have been the old days.

The music was patiently waiting for us to hear it again.

II

Though we know how far back the tradition of klezmer goes in Europe (earliest references are from around the 16th Century), we know more about the world in which the music existed than about the music itself.

Before the 19th Century the social fabric of the Jews of Europe was being stretched simultaneously in directions both West and East. In the West, on the one hand, came the rise of Moses Mendelssohn's enlightenment movement, known as Haskalah. It encouraged Jews to adopt the sociocultural traits of the non-Jewish society surrounding them, while also readjusting the religious rituals to accommodate these social adaptations. This resulted in the eventual replacement of various elements of traditional culture with essentially German ones. [1]

In Eastern Europe, on the other hand, Hasidism, under the guidance of the Ba'al Shem Tov, was coming alive. It strove to encourage Jews to express their piety in a way unacceptable up to that time: through the ecstatic fervor of music and dance. [2]

On the other hand, charismatic religiosity did not sit well with the more intellectual Misnagdim up north. Under the leadership of the Vilna Gaon, they stressed the values of scholarship and discipline and de-emphasized music and dance. The conflict between these three Jewish responses to modernity was destined to continue for many decades.

During these decades Jews who were used to living in small, out of the way towns found themselves uprooted by external developments. Changing borders and more liberal residency laws produced concomitant alterations in the cultural and economic condition of East European Jews, and prompted the relocation of many provincial Jews into the larger cities. The newly established laws which permitted (and in some cases conscripted) Jews to serve in the military were to have some ironically positive ramifications for some. [3]

Pogroms and rising anti-Semitic violence were the soiled ground from which grew the future movements of socialism and zionism; industrial, social and religious revolutions which were breaking out also contributed to the transformation of the traditional world of the Jews.

And in the midst of the historical turmoil was the klezmer trying to adapt to the changes.

The term klezmer comes from the Hebrew words "kley zemer" referring to the musical instruments themselves. At some point, however, the identities of the musician and his instrument merged to be covered by the one term "klezmer". In our own time, as we shall see, the term has stretched even further to include the whole musical genre. In addition to male klezmorim there is evidence of women playing klezmer music too.[4] Graphic images, such as painting and woodcuts available from the early days, show Jewish musicians playing instruments (and perhaps music) similar to those of their non-Jewish neighbors. It was this intimate interaction between both cultures that created an environment of eclecticism in Jewish music.

The rise of the Yiddish theatre in Rumania in the 1870's was to provide a fertile environment for Yiddish music to grow. However, just because this was theatre developed by Jews for Jews, it was far from devoid of non-Jewish influences. In his groundbreaking book Tenement Songs: *The Popular Music of the Jewish Immigrants* [5] musicologist Mark Slobin relates the following story about Abraham Goldfaden (1840-1908), the father of the Yiddish theatre. When auditioning prospective actor or singers for his company, Goldfaden would require an applicant to sing a song of his choice regardless of origin, be it Yiddish, operatic, sacred or secular. Unbeknownst to the auditionee, Arnold Perlmutter, Goldfaden's assistant, would be seated in a corner of the room copying the words and music to the songs. If the singer were chosen, he and his song were both included in the show, simultaneously expanded the musical mosaic of the play and creating a tight association between the song and singer. Of course, if the singer weren't chosen, at least Goldfaden had a new piece of music. Either way, he gave a broad musical education to his actors, musicians and audiences. Another by-product of Goldfaden's musical methodology was the codification of popular Yiddish folksong. By including his version of a widely known song, he essentially created a "definitive" version of it. This touring version by dint of its inclusion in a popular and highly mobile show gradually eclipsed many variants.

It was also in this period that the walls barring the entry of Jews into the rarified worlds of academia and classical music were scaled. For the first time, Jewish musicians could study, live and perform in locations previously closed to them without the painful necessity of conversion. So it was that a generation of wunderkinder like Mischa Elman became an inspiration to other musical Jews who could now dream of making the transition from kapelye (band) to concert hall.

The restrictions against the Jewish musicians, now slowly being lifted, had at one time been even more stringent. Alfred Sendry recounts in his Jewish Music in the Diaspora [6] numerous examples of the kinds of social stigmas that the klezmer endured in their respective countries. In 1641, for example, the Archbishop of Prague upheld a ruling allowing Jews the right to perform at non-Jewish functions on Sundays and holidays. However, due to the overwhelming negative response it evoked from professional non-Jewish musicians, the ruling was revoked. By 1648, nonetheless, the revocation was revoked, and in 1650, the revoked revocation was itself revoked. Later the next year, the final revocation was enacted. And again in 1652.

The circumstance of Jews playing for other Jews was also fraught with legal problems. In addition to arbitrary local laws making expensive permits a prerequisite for performance, there were also personnel quotas. In the Alsatian city of Metz, 3 musicians were allowed, while a fourth could only be added for a wedding. In Frankfurt, a quartet was allowed but had to quit by midnight. Sendry even cites the example of certain cities where on particular days klezmorim were forbidden to play at Jewish weddings. On the other hand, within the Jewish community the klezmer had to contend with religious disfavor. "They sought to erect a fence against hilarity..." is how Idelsohn described the actions of the rabonim, who sought to limit this potential for excess. Sendry also points out that, because many traditional weddings lasted from one to two weeks, it was necessary to hire non-Jewish musicians to play at those times when the Jewish musicians were proscribed by Jewish law.

Without a doubt, the best known milieu for the klezmer was the khasene (wedding). It was here that the musician most closely interacted with most of the members of his community. The klezmer played a specifically Jewish wedding repertoire, in addition to local peasant dance tunes. Literally, every step of the way was accompanied by the klezmer from the khosnmol, a party sponsored by the khosn (bridegroom) before the khasenes, to the sheve brokhes, played in honor of the khosn and kale (bride) the week after after the khupe (wedding ceremony). Throughout the wedding, specific dances for members of the family, friends and guests were played by the klezmorim (guests were obliged to pay the klezmorim for each dance they requested). Some of the wedding dances included the the badekns (veiling of the bride before the wedding), broyges tants (dance of anger and reconciliation), patsh tants (hand clapping dance), marches, khosid'ls, horas, "Russian" shers and doinas.

A form like the "Rumanian hora", for example (see "Gas Nign" or "Firn di Mekhutonim Aheym"), was commonly used as the musical accompaniment to escort older family members home after the conclusion of the wedding. Each dance had a particular purpose and place in the traditional wedding. [7]

It was the doina, not a dance tune, which was associated with the peak musical moment of the wedding. Because of its rhapsodic and expressive vocal quality (similar in feeling and modal structure to the singing of the khazn (cantor), this shepherd's lament from Rumania found great favor among Jews of Eastern Europe. The doina was the true test of a musician's oneness with his instrument whether it was playing a solo or accompanying the improvised wedding verses and commentary of the badkhn:

"The klezmorim in their seventies to nineties still remember the taksims (a type of free improvised form which has a great deal of scale and passage work which embellished the main theme of the piece; after such improvisation came a freylekhs in 2/4) were played. The younger klezmorim don't even recognize the concept of taksim; they have played doinas instead of taksims since the beginning of the twentieth century..." [8]

The Jewish musician was also a familiar figure at non-Jewish weddings. It was for both Jewish and gentile weddings that the klezmer developed the necessary flexibility of repertoires vital to serving broad musical needs. For the most part, the traditional Yiddish repertoire necessary for the Jewish wedding was inappropriate for a gentile one. Jewish musicians who were hired to play at non-Jewish parties were many times "requested" (i.e. demanded) to perform "typical" Jewish music in order to poke fun at it. One of the more popular tunes used was "Ma Yofus" (also called "Reb Dovidl's Nign" and "Tants, Tants Yidlekh"). So widespread was the phenomenon of this self satire that the players were referred to as "Ma Yofusniks(what one might call an "Uncle Tomashevsky") [9]. So even though typically Yiddish dances (such as the "Firn di Mekhutonim Aheym", contained elements of local folk music, they would not necessarily serve the same purpose at a gentile party.

But what of the non-Jewish repertoire played by the klezmer? For the most part it depended on the region and economic status of those who hired him. For all groups, a wide range of local peasant dances (polka, mazurka, hopak, etc.) was performed. The peasantry, however, would not usually demand more than this. It was among the local landowners and nobility that a more worldly repertoire was mandatory. In addition to classical and light classical works (such as Suppe's "Poet and Peasant" Overture) the klezmer was expected to play for popular salon dances (the waltz, quadrille and others). These genres of music were requested not long after their introduction among the more urbane nobility farther west. Other types of repertoire included local folk songs, religious hymns, ballads, and popular street songs.

In addition to Jewish and Gentile weddings, the klezmer could be found playing for a wide variety of other occasions. In the Jewish community there were occasional jobs playing for a bris (circumcision), the dedication of a new Torah scroll or shul (synagogue), or to accompany the Shabes klaper ("Sabbath banger") as he made his rounds reminding the townspeople to prepare for Shabes. Sendry also mentions the use of instrumental music in the shul before the services began on erev Shabes (Friday at dusk). For the community in general, there were also impromptu entertainments on market days, at fairs and in wine cellars. Some were hired to entertain in cafes, or during the summer season at spas and resorts. It was also possible to find work in the theatre (be it Yiddish or not), or even with a circus or a carnival. Of course, if the player were truly skilled or conservatory trained, it was possible to seek employment in symphony or opera orchestras; the success of finding a chair in an orchestra, of course, would have as much to do with the relative toleration for Jews in a particular time and place as with the player's ability. In every case, the Jewish musician was having to modify his abilities, his repertoire , and his expectations to fit the situation at hand. In some ways, this could be said to be the birth of the "club date" musician, a player who must blend the skills of an ethnomusicologist and a group psychologist: regardless of the type of entertainment, the klezmer was being challenged both to develop a wide repertoire and to make it sound like the one he was playing on any given occasion was the one he played best; he also had to second-guess his listeners of all persuasions, in order to play for them exactly what they wanted 3 minutes before they knew they wanted it.

One of the most fruitful interactions, and one whose mutual influences are still clear today, is the collaboration of Jews and Gypsies. Sharing as they did a common perception of Europe, independent of political boundaries, the musicians of both of these communities also shared an antipathy to the judgmental, heavy hand of other Europeans. Religion, mobility and quintessential "otherness", as well as a strong feeling for each other's music, did much to produce a meaningful musical symbiosis between these two ethnic minorities.

It was not only the repertoire the klezmer played that was constantly being changed, but also the instruments on which is was played. For example, those klezmer in Prague in the 1640's mentioned earlier would have played (when granted permission) on members of the violin family; fiddles, violas, and portable cellos (unlike Woody Allen's in "Take the Money and Run"). They also used flutes (fleytn), the baraban (drum),and a tsimbl (portable hammered dulcimer).It was the fidl (fiddle) that was the primary lead instrument, with the others playing counterpoints, harmonies or occasionally taking the melodic lead.

The predominance of the violin in the klezmer ensemble remained unchallenged until the relatively late introduction of the clarinet early in the 19th century. Both the violin and clarinet were evocative and mesmerizing instruments that sought out and found that most compelling aspect of the music: its closeness to the human voice. The music of the synagogue had a profound effect--both musically and emotionally--on the music of the klezmer. The khazn, as a representative of his community, spoke for and to its members, bringing out their deepest sense of identity. Ultimately what reached his community most effectively was both his command of both the prayers and his voice (so poignantly characterized by the use of the krekhtz (moan). One of my earliest childhood memories is of sitting in shul next to my mother in the women's section listening to my father conducting the Kol Nidre services. His singing so affected me that I turned to her and asked: "Farvos veynt der tate? "Why is daddy crying?" So it was with the klezmer. "He made his violin (or clarinet) laugh (or cry)" was more than poetic hyperbole --it really meant "He made ME laugh (or cry) with his violin (or clarinet)." What that was saying was that the musician's playing had reached that deepest part of the listener, the part that couldn't hide its feelings even if it wanted to. The laugh or cry of the music was really that of the community's own laughter or weeping coming back to it through the playing of the klezmer.

By the end of the 19th Century, brass instruments had been gradually introduced into klezmer bands. It is postulated that the rise of the brasses as a Yiddish instrument was due primarily to the increased presence of Jews in the various European armies. With the increased Jewish population in the army, more and more klezmer players (or even those who weren't) opted for,or were assigned to, military bands.[10] Perhaps not many of the surviving Yiddish band members returned home with their instruments, but they did go back with new musical knowledge and the opportunities in which to expand it. The increase of brasses may also have had something to do with the continued technological improvements of the instruments themselves. As newer, more modern instruments were introduced, the older ones became available to East European folk musicians who could then afford them.

It is important to keep in mind that the klezmer was not solely a resident of the shtetl, pictured by some as a quaint backwater town waiting to catch up to the 18th Century. The small agrarian villages so clearly evoked in the picturesque romantic images of "Fiddler on the Roof" or "Yentl" surely did exist -- but in fewer numbers than these movies would have us believe. Throughout Eastern Europe, Yiddish culture in all of its myriad forms could be found in large cities and small towns alike. It was no more unexpected to find a small, old fashioned klezmer band playing for change in a courtyard in a big city like Warsaw, than it was to come across a group of fervent young classical violinists in a town like Chelm (yes; there was a Chelm...)

The interaction between the Old World and the New was not unidirectional. There were numerous venues for those residents of Eastern Europe to gain access to ideas and events beyond their own particular regions. On the one hand publishing at this time was an enthusiastic industry and books of all sorts were being made available in ever increasing numbers. Publishing centers like Vilna and Warsaw issued volumes on every topic. Among these various types of books were collections of music which included popular dances, classical overtures and etudes. [11] The samples available to the Eastern European Jews were a combination of those published locally and those imported from the U.S. Combined with this was the emergence of Yiddish newspapers which catered to the plethora of Jewish world views from religious to revolutionary. The papers acted as a clearinghouse of political, cultural and ideological thought and helped to end provincialism.

In addition to the published music available to Yiddish players, the advent of recordings would soon change the soundscape of the klezmer. As early as 1897, recording studios were being set up throughout Europe that would eventually enable a klezmer from Poland to hear and learn the style of a klezmer from Belorussia (and later, one from America.) This would allow anyone who could afford it the luxury of listening at any time to the music of a traditional wedding without having to wait for the shadkhn (matchmaker) to do his job. The recording phenomenon was ultimately to have the effect both of preserving a particular musical style and of helping obscure its unrecorded variant forms forever by standardizing the performance, not unlike the effect Goldfaden earlier had on theatre music. Equally importantly, patrons would demand of their local klezmer that they "play it like on the record" establishing a "right" and "wrong" version rather than just "another" version. Though not everyone could afford records or a phonograph, the presence of merely one phonograph in a town was sufficient to help plant the seed for the de-regionalization of folk music. This situation was to continue to grow with the development of radio in the 1920's by offering music from even farther away which was free to boot. Records ,radio and printed music more than any other media, now would have a great effect on how the klezmer thought about and played his music.

III

The many reasons for the huge movement of Jews from Eastern Europe to the U.S. at the end of the 19th century have been the focus of a great deal of study. It is, however, not well documented how many, among the several million who came over between 1880-1924 were klezmorim. Because most, if not all, of our histories of the klezmer of this period come from recollections gathered in the last few years, we have a slightly skewed view of who came and why. For example, Joseph Frankel, a bandleader in the Czarist army, was on tour in the United States with the Russian Philharmonic and was stranded due to the outbreak of World War I. Like most people at that time, he figured the war would last a few weeks, so decided to wait it out. He waited until the outbreak of the Russian Revolution three years later and so made up his mind to stay permanently in the U.S. For the most part, however, this story is atypical.[12] Many of the klezmer who came here came of their own volition to escape the economic, social and religious oppression which was so rampant in Eastern Europe at that time. America, perceived as the "goldene medine" (golden land), may have been seen as a possible place to "make it" playing music, but not, for most, as a klezmer.

The lives of clarinetists Harry Kandel, Dave Tarras, and Naftule Brandwein are excellent cases in point. Kandel (1885-1943) was born in Cracow in 1885. How he came by his talents is not clear, as his family was not musical; his father ran a very successful lumber business. According to his daughter Doris Kandel, he applied to and was accepted by the Conservatory of Music in Odessa at an early age. It is also not clear if Kandel served in the Czarist Army band and had gone AWOL, or if he fled Russia prior to his induction. In any case, he came to the U.S. in 1905, and after landing in New York, found work almost immediately playing on the Keith Orpheum vaudeville circuit in "The Great Lafayette Band". After moving to Philadelphia, he played with John Philip Sousa's Band in a series of weekly concerts and tours, and by 1916, was leading a dance band in Atlantic City under the name "Harry Kandel's Famous Inlet Orchestra".

But this wasn't klezmer music.

It wasn't until 1917, 12 years after his arrival, that Kandel actually began his career in Jewish music, recording several discs for the Victor Record Company in nearby Camden, New Jersey. Suddenly, Kandel found himself leading Victor's most prolific Yiddish orchestra. [13] In many ways, Kandel was the linchpin of the Philadelphia klezmer scene which also containedsuch fine Yiddish players as the outstanding percussionist Jacob ("Jake") Hoffman,[14]clarinetist Itzikl Kramtweiss (see 'Baym Rebin in Palestina"), and such fiddlers and bandleaders as Kol Katz (uncle of a current klezmer bandleader, Hankus Netsky of the Klezmer Conservatory Band). In 1927, 10 years to the month after his first recording session, Kandel abruptly quit music, went into the retail appliance business (ostensibly also to sell Victrolas and records) and never played again.

The circumstances of Dave Tarras, born in 1897, was somewhat different. As a child in the Ukrainian town of Ternovka, he exhibited a great musical aptitude. He rapidly progressed from balalaika to mandolin to flute and finally, to clarinet. His father, a trombonist and band leader, gave him his earliest training, which was later augmented with the experience of playing in a Czar Nikolai military band. However, when Tarras came to America in 1921, he could not even conceive of the possibility of being able to play music here. He said: " I thought that in America to be a musician, one has to have...he has to be something. I didn't think I'm good enough to be a musician..." [15]

(There was also another problem: upon his arrival at Ellis Island, Tarras' bags, which included his clothes and clarinet, were all fumigated. His clothes survived. His clarinet didn't.) He was soon hired as a cutter in his cousin's furrier shop where he worked until another cousin took him along to play some weddings. Within a short time, word got out to the Yiddish music scene that there was a terrific new greenhorn clarinetist, one to rival the reigning "King of Jewish Music", clarinetist Naftule Brandwein.

Brandwein (1889-1963) was a very colorful and fiery player whose highly individualistic style made him thrilling to hear and difficult to work with. He came to the U.S. around 1913 and, unlike the aforementioned Kandel and Tarras, quickly established a name for himself in the American Jewish music scene. In 1917, Brandwein was hired by bandleader Abe Schwartz to play in his ensemble, which recorded for Columbia records. He continued as a section player until 1922 when he made his first solo records. It was not much later that Tarras arrived.

There is much about the life of Naftule Brandwein to warrant the term "legendary." The stories about him range from his having performed on-stage wearing an Uncle Sam costume made entirely of Xmas tree lights and very nearly electrocuting himself with his own perspiration, to his being the favorite musician of Brooklyn's notorious "MurderInc." to his playing on stage with his back to the audience so no one could steal his ideas (this last story is true by all accounts, even though, one might ask, if Brandwein didn't want anyone "stealing" his ideas, why did he make so many records...?)

On top of all this, he couldn't read music.

Tarras, with his dignified professional mien, easily became the preferred clarinetist for performer, composer and audience alike. He has since come to occupy a unique place in American klezmer music as the model for several generations of American born Jewish clarinetists due to his elegant, clean and precise manner of performance as well as his numerous compositions, which have become classics of the style.

Tarras has continued his involvement in music to the present day,and was a recipient of the prestigious National Heritage Folklife Award from the National Endowment of the Arts in 1984.

Though Brandwein enjoyed one brief return to recording in 1942, he continued playing weddings and at Catskills hotels; only with this recent reinterest in klezmer has his music finally been re-evaluated as it deserves.

IV

By the time the klezmer players came to America, there were numerous musical options open both in and out of the Jewish community. On the one hand, American popular entertainment had been steadily growing. Vaudeville had taken hold after years of the minstrel shows popularity. Those players who could read and play well found making the transition into mainstream American musical life through vaudeville easier than their musically illiterate colleagues.The music they were playing, however, was not Jewish. In fact, the kind of "ethnic" representation found on the American stage at that time was on the order of the earlier minstrel shows and Irish "Mulligan" plays, but with a broader range of "depictable exotic types". [16] It was ironic, that some Jewish musicians found themselves playing accompaniments to men who were parodying them by singing songs like "Yankl, the Cow-Boy Jew", or "When Mose With His Nose Leads the Band".

Yiddish theatre began its rise in the U.S. in the 1880's, along with the first wave of the Eastern European migration. The popular and artistic offerings which were presented to the immigrant Yiddish audience spanned the full range from broad comedies to avant- garde experimental Stanislavskian theatre, with audiences for all. This panorama of possibilities provided a wide range of actors, singers, composers, playwrights and musicians with the forum in which to create the genre. Composers like Joseph Rumshinsky, Herman Wohl, Arnold Perlmutter (the one who had transcribed for Goldfaden), Alexander Olshanetsky, Sholom Secunda, and singers like Aaron Lebedeff, Molly Picon, Maurice Schwartz, Gus Goldstein, and Sam Kasten, among many others, helped create a distinctive American Yiddish musical theatre. Many of the composers, for example, began their professional careers in Europe as meyshoyr'rim. Meshoyr'rim were apprentice khazonim, learning the modes, scales, articulations and seasonal usages of various kinds of melodies to the same texts. They had already learned about the subtle interaction of presentations both physical and musical in that most powerful of Jewish theatres: the synagogue. In essence, then, what they did was to adapt the drama, music and familiarity of the synagogue performance in order to come to grips with the conflict of the new American environment. It was in Yiddish theatre in collaboration with many of the above mentioned composers and singers that musicians like Dave Tarras and Shloimke Beckerman found a great bulk of their work.

Of course, weddings were still the "flanken and potatoes" of the Jewish musician's work. While Jewish immigration was on the rise, catering halls began springing up in the various Yiddish enclaves around the city from the Lower East Side of Manhattan to Brooklyn's Brownsville to the Bronx's Grand Concourse. In the transition from Europe to the U.S. immigrant musicians now played more fox trots than freylekhs and used contemporary instruments such as the saxophone and the tenor banjo. Of course it was still possible to find a wedding in which the older ritual dances (such as the patsh tants, broyges tants) were still part of the ceremonial progression. It was easier, however, to find a badkhn, than a job for him; both traditional practices and the Yiddish language itself were falling into increasing disfavor among young American Jews. In addition, bar mitzvahs became larger and larger affairs whereas in the past the receptions had been simple kiddushim after the services. Other musical outlets were the development of the various landsmanshaftn, (regional fraternal organizations) which regularly sponsored dinners and dancing, as well as numerous fund-raisers for newspapers, political aspirants and social causes. With the rise of the Catskill region of upstate New York as a popular vacation area for immigrant Jews, musicians found many places to play in bands for the summer and on holidays like Passover. In essence, then, though the American Jewish milieu had produced many new and different performance opportunities, the involvement of the klezmer with the community had not changed.Other jobs in both the Jewish and non-Jewish worlds included playing at the numerous cafes, roof garden restaurants, cabarets, and theatres throughout the city. A musician, like cymbalist Joseph Moskowitz also owned their own restaurants, his being "Moskowitz and Lupowitz" on the Lower East Side. [17].

The emergence of radio also offered an excellent showcase for the diverse talents of players and music readers like Dave Tarras and Shloimke Beckerman. With the increase of the number of Yiddish speaking Jews, radio sought to cater to the needs of the community. Several stations like WHN and WBBC had some kind of Yiddish programming, only radio station WEVD, owned by the Yiddish daily the "Forverts" and named for the unsuccessful two-time Socialist Presidential contender, Eugene Victor Debs had broad popular Jewish programming. Many of the successful Yiddish theatre composers also wrote music for the dramas, musicals, game shows and soap operas which appeared on the air, in addition to those musical programs which spotlighted their own talents.

Despite all these live performing outlets for the Jewish musician, it was the recording industry that was to be both a source of work for the klezmer and an important tool for future generations of musicians who would hear exactly what their predecessors sounded like. [18] But it is important to note that neither the commercial record companies nor the musicians were concerned about "preservation" of the music at the time. The record companies were interested in the exploitation of those eager markets which were willing to purchase recordings of their own ethnic performers in numbers sufficiently large to warrant the companies' investment and to ensure a profit. These records were kept in the catalogs so long as they sold; if they did not, they were dropped. The musicians, on the other hand, also thought nothing of "preservation" or of recording as a bid for lasting fame. They were simply playing music for their community as they had always done; old music, which was still popular, and new popular music which was created in abundant amounts. Now, the recording studio had simply been added to the other contexts in which they played.

The earliest recordings of Jewish music were made in America around 1898. Although the great majority of them were of khazonim and Yiddish theatre singers, over 700 klezmer records were issued between the years 1894-1942. The majority of these records was issued between the years 1913-1930 and centered on the sales of a handful of prolific performers. The competition between the record labels was stiff. Except for the issues from the short-lived "United Hebrew Disc and Cylinder Record Company" (UHD&C) (1905-06), all recordings were made by general record companies. [19] Columbia Records, for example, signed composer and violinist Abe Schwartz in New York to record some discs for them in early 1917. By the end of the year Victor in Camden, New Jersey countered by signing Philadelphia based Harry Kandel. In December of that same year Kandel recorded "Der Shtiler Bulgar" and the following September, Columbia had Abe Schwartz (under the nom de disque "Jewish Orchestra") re-record it. Other groups who rose to the recording occasion were bands headed by Abe Ellenkrig (who recorded the first "modern" klezmer records), Al Glaser, Israel J. Hochman, Abe Katzman, Max Leibowitz, Alexander Olshanetsky, Art Shryer, Simkha ("Sam") Young and Abe Weissman. Soloists included violinist Jacob Gegna, clarinetists

Shloimke Beckerman, Philip Greenberg and Max Weissman, cymbalist Joseph Moskowitz and accordionists Nathan Hollander and Mishka Ziganoff, among others.

On none of the recordings of this period, however, does one find the word klezmer or klezmorim, in the various band names. It is only the recent return to this music which revived and glorified this name (though Beregovski first uses the term "klezmer music" in his 1937 essay on the genre, it was probably the Argentinian born clarinetist Giora Feidman who popularized the term). In the era in which the 78's were made the appellation was still considered "backwoods", and not at all complimentary. According to Pete Sokolow: " In those days they never called this 'klezmer music'. They called it 'the bulgars'...A klezmer was what they called somebody who couldn't play anything but the old Jewish tunes. It was a derogatory term." [20].

These 78's have become, for the most part, the equivalent of "3 minute musical Rosetta Stones", offering latter day klezmer players a chance to decode the musical messages of an earlier era. But how true to life are the messages? The acoustic and length limitations inherently found on the early disks forced the musicians to adjust what they were offering. For example, the earliest recording method, the"acoustic" process (wherein a musician played directly into a horn, not a microphone,) had severe limitations in terms of which instruments it could pick up clearly. The earliest klezmer 78's featured 19th century instrumental pairings such as fiddle or flute accompanied by the tsimbl (hammered dulcimer), whose gentle sound was later drowned out by the larger brass bands. Soon, pianos substituted for tsimbls, tubas for string basses and brasses outpowered strings. Even with the development in 1925 of the "electrical" process (which did use a microphone and produced a superior sound), the ensemble structure was not appreciably altered. This represented the instrumental sound which was common to all types of music being recorded at the time and may account for some listeners hearing a "klezmer" sound on jazz and pop 78's and even animated cartoon soundtracks! Recordings also raise the question as to the nature of what constituted a "tune". As indicated by older klezmorim, the concept of a "tune" as an autonomous and singular entity ran counter to standard performance practice. A string of melodies had always been combined to accompany dancers for dance sets lasting from 20 minutes to half an hour. It is possible then, that for the non-musical reasons of disc length (about 3 minutes for a 10" 78 and 4 minutes for a 12") and marketing considerations (each new catalog had to have new tunes and new titles to sell), a new relationship was forged between the musician and his music. Melodies had to be surgically separated and each 48 measures needed to be codified and named separately. Up until this point, tunes had been referred to by their attendant dance name, and not by a separate title. [21]

In addition to the recordings there was also a related field: music publishing. Sheet music of popular songs published by journeymen printers start turning up almost as early as newspapers and books. The largest printer of Jewish music was the Hebrew Publishing Company which issued hundreds of titles. The overwhelming majority of the sheets was, like the records, Yiddish theatre and cantorial material but with occasional individual klezmer pieces. A few independent publishers actually did print klezmer collections. As with the recording of Jewish music, the first known commercial exploitation of the music was instigated from outside the community. Publisher Carl Fischer, better known for his popular and classical publications, issued the first collection of Yiddish instrumental music in 1912. This was followed in 1916 by the brothers Kostakowsky who published "Celebrated Hebrew Wedding Dances" and other small collections.

It was however, the 1924 publication of "The International Dance Folio" series by Jack and Joseph Kammen which produced the first popular anthology. Billed as "The Most Useful Book of Its Kind", the Kammen books (only volumes 1 and 9 are still available), preserved some of the old repertoire in a simplified form.

But in this simplified form, for whom could it have been meant?

The older players would have already internalized this repertoire, while for the younger players the book gave no sense of phrasing, ornamentation or style. As clarinetist Sid Beckerman told me about the books: "Those who could play the music didn't need the books and those who needed the books couldn't play the music." Or as another put it more bluntly: "Admitting that you learned to play (Jewish) from a book, was like admitting you learned how to have sex from a manual!" The bandstand was considered the only proper way to learn repertoire and style, and not the place for page turning.

The huge catalog of wedding tunes, hasidic-inspired melodies, and instrumental renderings of cantorial or religious music were now joined by settings of popular Yiddish theatre songs, and updated arrangements of old time music. This was also a period of reconciliation between modern and traditional musical values. A good example was Joseph Cherniavsky who with his "Yiddish American Jazz Band" cut a path between Jewish and American entertainment. From 1923-1925, he featured such players as Naftule Brandwein, Dave Tarras, Shloimke Beckerman and Joe Helfenbein, who appeared both in Yiddish theatres and on the vaudeville circuit dressed as Hasidim or Cossacks (both exotic images in the United States). They performed and recorded contemporary arrangements of traditional klezmer music and newly written music by Cherniavsky meant to have the sense of the old. In 1925, Cherniavsky recorded a suite of melodies composed for An-sky's drama "The Dybbuk" in 1926, Jack Mills, a popular music publisher, issued these and other tunes taken from Cherniavsky's recent Victor releases; this piano reduction --Cherniavsky used 13 musicians-- was obviously meant for home and not bandstand use.) Though they called themselves "Jazz" the band was composed of mainstream Jewish performers. As with many European born klezmer, Cherniavsky's players had little or no contact with the worlds in which jazz was growing; neither finally, did they have the flexibility to adapt. There were, of course, musicians like Harry Raderman who played trombone in both klezmer bands (such as Shloimke Beckerman's) and with the "High Hatted Tragedian of Jazz" Ted Lewis (Theodore Leopold Friedman), but this was not so much jazz as it was jazz-influenced popular music. Or to borrow a sociolinguistic analogy, the presence of a foreign-born speaking accent in a way indicated the presence of a musical one, one which may have the blocked entry into the innovative avant garde of jazz. [22]

It was the Jewish musicians born here, the second generation klezmer, who would ultimately benefit from the influence of jazz. On the one hand, this was the birth of the club date musician in American Jewish life, the all purpose player who could "cover" a Jewish call and also play the popular music of the time. The younger players born here internalized the nuance of American language and music more acutely than the older klezmorim while retaining some Yiddish musical "accent"---and thereby continued the eclectic tradition of bi-musicality. What a freylekhs was to the father a fox trot was to the son. On the other hand, someone like Benny Goodman (1909-1986) came to represent to the 1930's American Jewish community what Mischa Elman had to an earlier European generation: a Jew who could make it in the non-Jewish world playing non-Jewish music and not have to convert to do it. Goodman, however, did not play Jewish music. It was his star trumpet player Ziggy (Harry Finkleman) Elman (1914-1968) who introduced and played the "Jewish" solos in the orchestra. This misconception has fostered the impression that Goodman played "klezmer", which he never claimed to do. Another excellent example of a talented musician on both the big band and klezmer scenes was clarinetist and saxophonist Sam Musiker. Musiker (1924-1967) was, as his name implies, from a musical tradition. He played klezmer and popular music as a child and at age 18 joined drummer Gene Krupa, late of the Goodman band. It was there that he learned the rudiments of big band composition and arrangement. After the war, Musiker turned to the playing and recording of klezmer music. He, along with brother Ray and father-in-law Dave Tarras, organized, arranged and played the most innovative and brilliant klezmer/jazz fusion to that time. The pairing was, however not to take hold. A combination of the passing of big bands, plummeting record sales, and the changing tastes in the American Jewish community combined to limit growth in this direction.

These changing tastes had been in rapid motion since 1924, when large scale Jewish emigration to America was closed by the U.S. government. This narrowed the potential markets for old time Yiddish music here, even though there was still a healthy transatlantic exchange of theatre companies, records and sheet music. The increased acculturation of Yiddish folkways and Yankee fashions was further motivated by a firm belief in the melting pot scenario. More and more young Jewish artists, writers, professionals and musicians strove to make it in the outside world. In those years between the end of World War II and the 1960's the Jewish community adapted a completely new view of its cultural identity in response to the devastation of the Holocaust and the birth of the state of Israel. Despite the elimination of a vast portion of traditional European Jewish life, there was still less an urge to develop what remained of Yiddish culture than that of Israel. Slowly, the American Jewish community developed a dual sense of identity: on the one hand a pride in the new State, and the adoption of an essentially nostalgic view of the "Old Country" on the other. In fact, the concept of what constituted the "Old Country" also began to change. As children married and moved to more upscale locations the "Old Neighborhood" became the new "Old Country", substituting Chrystie Street for Kasrilivke.

With this expanded identity, the music soundscape changed again. The non-Jewish repertoire now included more Latin music (the cha-cha now joined or replaced the earlier tango) but also rock'n'roll was increasingly requested for weddings and bar mitzvahs. In addition, when someone asked for something "Jewish" they could just as easily mean a song of the Palestinian halutzim (pioneers) as a song of the Yiddish theatre. The identification of "Israeli=Jewish" was also clearly reflected in the blossoming of Israeli folk dance. When folk dance troupes and clubs did "Jewish" dances, the majority were Israeli, thereby replacing the "hora" (3/8 time) with the "hora" (2/4 time). It was not only the repertoire which had changed, but the instrumentation, too. The clarinet, which had displaced the violin as *the* "Jewish" instrument was itself now displaced in the new world of Israeli music (by its old partner, the accordion, and the "chalil"(recorder). As Israeli popular music ultimately succeeded in emulating American popular music in the 1960's and 70's, its rock and pop oriented emphasis obviated the need to include these now old fashioned instruments. It had become easier to be both Jewish and modern, a very important consideration for emerging Jewish youth.

But the post-war years also saw Jews coming into the U.S. in the largest numbers since 1924. This influx of refugees from the old world helped to stem the decline of old style Yiddish music on the contemporary American scene. These grine (greenhorns) (which includes my family) like all grine before them needed their old world culture during the process of adjusting to the new world.

Because their spiritual centers were all in Europe, the great majority of Hasidim did not come to America until after those centers had been destroyed by the war. With their arrival came the development of the Hasidic market as a new and vibrant field (unlike the 1920's, when non-Hasidic groups like Cherniavsky's Yiddish-American Jazz Band portrayed "Hasidim" to other non-Hasidim, thus producing a kind of in-group minstrel show) these were musicians playing real Hasidic music for real Hasidim. The first Hasidic-scene bandleader, Joe King, along with clarinetists like Max Epstein and Rudy Tepel (who among other clarinetists of this era were very influenced by Dave Tarras), and tenor saxaphonist Howie Leess, came to epitomize and define Hasidic music in America. It was in these years that Hasidic and klezmer music was played in a more similar style to each other than they are today. Hasidic music, as Israeli music did before it, has largely abandoned the more "Yiddish" parts of the ensemble (though a clarinetist who plays in a Rudy Tepel style is occasionally heard), and has adopted a popular electric sound producing such hybrids as "HasiDisco" and "OrthoRock" music.

The outlets for Jewish music had also been slowly changing in the post-war period. The glory days of the Yiddish theatre were over, as theatre after theatre closed. In addition, there were too few actors, actresses, writers or composers to carry on the work that of those who had passed on. [23]

Catskills hotels were also beginning their slow decline as the preferred vacation place for the Jewish community. Other traditional outlets like radio, with WEVD left as the only station still offering Yiddish (and soon being forced to sell off its AM station) had already cut back on the amount of live playing and going more for recorded music. And even so, the amount of recording and issuing of this music had also hit an all time low. Some Jewish-owned labels, like "Banner", "Asch", "Tikvah", and "Collector's Guild", still offered Jewish records (both newly recorded and re-issues); a few, such as "Collector's Guild", still produced a superior product in packaging and production.

As can be imagined, the older klezmer repertoire was constantly diminishing in size. Certain dance forms had already disappeared as their social function faded. The badkhn was also gone from the general Jewish wedding (though he remains to this day in the Hasidic world). It was unlikely to find weddings where the band played a patsh tants unless asked (and some bands might have to look it up in the Kammen folio.) Fewer and fewer people knew the dances; thus the functional connection between them had been severed. The music had become more of a nostalgia stimulator with the musician cutting back on the scope of his repertoire; it was becoming unnecessary, for example, for a player to need more than one Yiddish theatre medley or doina at a wedding. In fact, even the saxophone had become a more important reed instrument to have on the bandstand than a clarinet. Because of its use on foxtrots, waltzes, standards and even rock'n'roll it had become more functional and versatile than the clarinet.

The repertoire, instrumentation, function, and frequency of performance of klezmer music was in a severe decline; players such as Dave Tarras, Sid Beckerman, Max Epstein, Rudy Tepel (who played at my Bar-Mitzvah) Marty Levitt and Pete Sokolow continued to include some klezmer music at every wedding, despite an all time low interest.

It was the age of "Jewzak".

But this is where we came in.

V

After my bar mitzvah, my interest in Jewish music was also at an all time low. I left yeshiva and entered a new world. I eventually drifted into the folk songs of Woody Guthrie, Cisco Houston and Bob Dylan. I found myself getting into more traditional kinds of music: Irish tunes, New England contra dances and primarily Appalachian string band music.

In the summer of 1973, I went with a few friends down to Surry County North, Carolina. We went to visit with and learn from Tommy Jarrell, a 73 year old master of traditional American music. Tommy's expansive generosity was equal to his skill with a fiddle and banjo.

I was called Hank then. And I played traditional Appalachian music.

A couple of years later on my third visit to Mt. Airy (birthplace of Andy Griffith and model for TV's "Mayberry"), Tommy asked me something. He had always known that there was an extraordinarily high percentage of young Jews playing old time music. He didn't understand it, but he accepted it. One day he asked me in all candor: "Hank, don't your people got none of your own music?" It just seemed strange to him that here were all these talented musicians coming down to play his traditional music and play it well. Where was their own people's music?

Where, indeed?

On my zeyde's (grandfather's) advice, I started my research by calling the YIVO Institute for Jewish Research in New York. Without trying hard, I reached folklorist Barbara Kirshenblatt-Gimblett who invited me down to see the music collection. When I first visited the record collection I was thrilled! Austen Henry Layard couldn't have been any more excited unearthing the palaces of Nineveh, then I was opening those cabinets full of 78's. Hundreds and hundreds of records. My first great revelation was that these 78's were of similar vintage to the ones I was learning old time country music from. The same pops. The same scratches. The same ancient, far away sound that made the image of opening a long sealed crypt so appealing. (I now realized the mistake I'd made some years earlier in letting those Jewish "Orchestra" records go.) The more I listened to this music the more I realized that this is what I was trying to run away from. But it sounded different somehow. Somehow, the music of the Catskills, the sound of my father's voice, and the Lubavitch schoolbus became new to me; it was all rolled into one but now had a great, unselfconscious feeling---the same thing I found in hillbilly music. What was different was that this music was mine. It was then I had another revelation:Tommy Jarrell and my zeyde, Isaac Steinberg, were the same age.

It wasn't long after that I received a response to a letter I'd written to musicologist Mark Slobin. He mentioned that I should contact someone he'd just met in California who was recording a new album of klezmer music: Lev Liberman of "The Klezmorim". I contacted him and vacationed on the West Coast that summer. To say that we greeted each other like long lost brothers is an understatement. We each thought that we were laboring in a vacuum and that no one would understand what we were doing. Along with full-time linguist and part-time musicologist Dr. Martin Schwartz and clarinetist David Julian Gray, we spent the summer listening to klezmer 78's, making copies, reading transcriptions, arguing over instrumentation, and generally taking great pleasure in the hour by hour discoveries we were making. What a pleasure it was to meet them.

I returned to New York inspired.

The next year I started full-time klezmer research on a grant from the government, at the Martin Steinberg Center of the American Jewish Congress just around the corner from the YIVO. I couldn't believe I was getting paid to do this. My days were spent haunting the halls at YIVO playing records, translating ads and articles from the Yiddish and going around to senior centers giving lectures all the while hoping to meet some old klezmorim. One day it happened. I was giving a talk at a YM/YWHA in the Bronx and mentioned Joseph Cherniavsky's group when a woman in the second row laughed and said her husband played with him.

"Is...is your husband in good health?", I asked.

"Yeah!" she said "He was when I left him in the other room playing pinochle."

That's how I met Joe Helfenbein, Joseph Cherniavsky's drummer.

In early 1979, I received a call at the Steinberg Center asking if it were possible for me to organize a klezmer band for a concert in Providence, R.I. that November.

I didn't know if it was possible, but I was anxious to find out.

I went poking around looking for folks who might be interested in playing in such a band. Within a short time Josh Waletzky, Michael Alpert, Lauren Brody, Ken Maltz and Dan Conte had joined me in "Kapelye". We played the show and scored our first success. (Dan Conte left not long after and was replaced with Eric Berman. Josh also eventually left, but he remains irreplaceable.)

In 1981, on the recommendation of my mentor Barbara Kirshenblatt-Gimblett, I was hired to organize a national touring Yiddish show, called "Der Yidisher Caravan". Along with the members of "Kapelye", clarinetist Andy Statman, my father and the late David Ellin, among others, we toured the U.S. We played old time klezmer music, Yiddish theatre and cantorial songs to thousands of enthusiastic people from Portland east to Portland west.

There were others playing the music. In New York clarinetist and mandolinist Andy Statman (also a veteran of the New York country music scene) and tsimblist Zev Feldman had been playing old time klezmer music for awhile. They were, in conjunction with the Balkan Arts Center, responsible for staging the first Dave Tarras klezmer music extravaganza in 1978. What a surprise for everyone (not the least Dave himself) that there were scores of people interested in this music. (I was reminded not long afterwards that my father and Dave Tarras were old friends from the Catskill days and had provided the guests with the full gamut of Jewish music between them.) Andy has since gone on to play using various types of accompaniments. In Boston, jazz instructor Hankus Netsky organized a real Yiddish big band (recreating the sound of the 13 piece bands on the 78's) made up of Conservatory talent. Soon he had the "Klezmer Conservatory Band".

After several years of research, I produced the first re-issue of period 78 recordings, entitled "Klezmer Music:1910-1942" for Folkways. This was a truly collaborative effort on the part of the cutting edge of the klezmer scene including Dr. Martin Schwartz, Lev Liberman, Andy Statman and Zev Feldman. The next year saw my YIVO wanderings finally came to an end. With a generous grant from the members of the Weinstein family, I was asked by YIVO to design and direct the "Max and Frieda Weinstein Archives of Recorded Sound". Those records which I had first seen on my initial visit to the YIVO were now the core of the newest archives dedicated to traditional music.

In the summer of 1982, Kapelye was hired to appear and play in the Hollywood film version of Chaim Potok's novel "The Chosen". The irony was not lost on me that here I was portraying a hasid, a role I played during the major chunk of my "Wonder Years". Kapelye and Pete Sokolow (who also appears in the film with us) have never ceased to be amazed at how many people we meet who had their first exposure to klezmer music because of this film. (The Klezmorim and Andy Statman later also went on to record soundtracks for films). Shortly after we completed the film, we issued our first album.

The first re-issue. A Hollywood film. A new album.

This was it. We hit the top.

Not quite.

By this time, The Klezmorim were playing to ever widening audiences in all sorts of locations, and exposing greater numbers of people to klezmer. Lev, Marty and myself, when we could find the time, used to swap cassettes of records that we'd recently stumbled across (it was from Lev that I had gotten my copy of the rare Kostakowsky book.) Not long after that, Marty Schwartz came out with his excellent klezmer reissue, "Klezmer Music 1910-1926". We were like kids in a candy store. In March of 1983 Andy Statman and I were asked by New York's Jewish Museum to produce a show called "Klezmer Meets Jazz", which was based on a lecture/demonstration I organized through the Steinberg Center with Nat Hentoff and David Amram. Along with Pete Sokolow and some of the top New York Jewish and jazz players we played two sold out performances there and another at Joseph Papp's Public theatre. After the run of the show, Pete kept the arrangements he wrote and used them to organize the Original Klezmer Jazz Band, recording an album in 1984.

It was also that same year that "The Klezmorim" played Carnegie Hall, which did much to raise the general consciousness of klezmer music among a wider audience. Not only that, but Hankus' "Klezmer Conservatory Band" enjoyed a great success premiering klezmer music on Garrison Keillor's hit NPR radio show "A Prairie Home Companion", opening a whole new territory ("Kapelye" played the show a few seasons later.) In the summer of 1984 we became the first American klezmer band to tour Europe. Our itinerary included Britain, France, Switzerland, Belgium and Germany. We were gratified to receive an enthusiastic reaction wherever we performed. Europe has since served as host to Andy Statman and The Klezmorim. (The most bizarre irony of our tour occurred in Berlin. We were booked for three nights at a cafe called the "Einstein" which was housed in a breathtaking turn-of-the-century mansion built for a Jewish owner. On our last night we were made privy to the "biography of the building": among other owners, this building was used as the provisional HQ of the Gestapo during the war.)

Carnegie Hall. A Sound Archives. A European tour. I couldn't believe there was more.

There was.

Word started filtering through the klezmer grapevine that there were new bands forming in places like Seattle, Washington; Albuquerque, New Mexico; New Orleans, Louisiana; Boulder, Colorado; Portland, Oregon and Montpelier, Vermont: places you don't usually connect with Yiddish culture. But klezmer seemed to be going where the Jews were. Suddenly, the idea of a real coast-to-coast klezmer community seemed possible. More than possible: it has happened!

Years before, I had been on the staff of a music camp which catered to people who wanted to learn Appalachian music from experienced professionals. I figured if there could be a camp for old time country music, there could be a camp for old time klezmer music. So, I organized, along with the YIVO and with the assistance of folks in the klezmer scene, what has since become the annual "Yiddish Folk Arts Program", first held in the Catskills in the middle of Hanukah 1985. "Klez Kamp", as it came to be called, brought together some of the most enthusiastic teachers and over 130 folks from all around the country who had come to play klezmer music. Dance to it. Learn Yiddish. And meet the older, experienced carriers of the Yiddish traditions. Not too long ago you could count the number of klezmer bands on the fingers of one hand. Now you'd need 8 hands to do it. Some of the finest players on the klezmer scene were there on staff including Hankus Netsky, Stuart Brotman, Joel Rubin, Pete Sokolow, Mimi Rabson, and Michael Alpert, not to mention folk-arts specialists like Barbara Kirshenblatt-Gimblett, Mark Slobin and Lee Ellen Friedland. One of the greatest thrills was introducing veteran clarinetist Sid Beckerman to a new world of youthful, enthusiastic players who greatly valued the gift he shared with them. Almost as much as he enjoyed sharing it with them. The culture which was mourned as lost was being celebrated by a whole new generation of practitioners.

And that's all there is.

(Or is it...?)

Henry Sapoznik
January 1987

NOTES

[1]   Ironically, the Jewish wedding was later to have appended to it music composed by the grandson of the Haskalah's founder. The Wedding March from Felix Mendelssohn's "Midsummer Night's Dream" has become a standard of ceremonial wedding music. Mendelssohn, incidentally, was present at a concert of the great klezmer, Michael Josef Gusikow (1806?-1837) in 1836. Gusikow, who played the "shtroyfidl", a kind of xylophone on a bed of straw, was a well known virtuoso. Mendelssohn was so moved by Gusikow's talents , that he wrote to his mother praising the player and "his national music" (not remembering that at one time not long before it had been Mendelssohn's "national music", too.)

[2]   This resulted in the establishment of a very powerful presence of music in all its forms in Hasidic life. This ranged from the inclusion of the simple and poignant nigun (wordless song) into everyday activities, to the founding of extravagant klezmer orchestras in residence for some of the larger, more powerful Hasidic courts.

[3]   Though Jewish recruits suffered at the hands of other recruits and officers (not to mention the enemy), Jewish musicians were offered something many of them couldn't receive back home: the chance to learn to read and write music and to play in a disciplined "Western" ensemble.

[4]   A.Z. Idelsohn: *Jewish Music in Its Historical Development.* New York: Schocken 1967

[5]   University of Indiana Press 1982

[6]   Alfred Sendry *Music Of the Jews in the Diaspora.* New York Philosophical Library 1969

[7]   Though there is no re-interest in the dance world comparable to the scope of the musical klezmer revival, quality original fieldwork in dance reconstruction and documentation has been accomplished by dance ethnographers such as Lee Ellen Friedland and Jill Gellerman.

[8]   Beregovski, Moshe: "Jewish Instrumental Folk Music" reprinted in "Old Jewish Folk Music" Mark Slobin, ed. Philadelphia, University of Pennsylvania Press 1982) This article, published in Kiev in 1937 was a prelude to a much larger work, the first serious call for the systematic and in depth study of the klezmer his repertoire and his life. The hopeful and enthusiastic tone of Beregovski's article is tragic in retrospect given the events which occurred only a short time after its writing in 1937. The completed volume, according to the Soviet Yiddish magazine

"Sovietish Heimland" is claimed to exist in the Soviet Union, which plans to issue it shortly. Bringing this volume to light has also been the goal of scholars such as Slobin and Prof. Robert Rothstein.

[9]   See notes to Ma Yofus "Klezmer Music 1910-1926" Folklyric 9054 by Martin Schwartz

[10]   This was the case with players like Dave Tarras and Harry Kandel.

[11]   Clarinetist Dave Tarras recalls that as a child growing up in the Ukrainian town of Ternovka, he was too poor to afford a subscription to the latest published music, but an uncle of his did receive one and shared the music with his eager nephew then.

[12]   See notes to "Jakie, Jazz 'em Up" GVM 101

[13]   The large majority of Jewish instrumental records had knowledgeable Yiddish players; on the other hand, many musical accompaniments for the Yiddish singers and comics were recorded by regular house bands which didn't necessarily have any idea of Yiddish style, beyond what was found in the arrangements. Victor, for example, did not have Kandel accompany its roster of Yiddish theatre stars, but leaders like Rosario Bourdon, Edward King and Nathaniel (Nat) Shilkret.

[14]   See "Klezmer Music 1910-1926" Folkyric 9034 and "Jakie, Jazz'em Up" GVM 101 for examples of his playing;

[15]   See notes to "Klezmer Music 1910-1942" Folkways FSS 34021.

[16]   Racial and ethnic stereotyping abounded on the American stage in this period, portraying many minority groups in a one dimensional manner and thus producing mountains of malicious material. These portrayals were not meant to be viewed or appreciated by the groups represented; mainstream American audiences expected portrayals which vindicated their negative or naive opinions of ethnic and racial groups. For the most part the performers portraying the "type" were not members of that group (exceptions were the black singer/comedian Bert Williams and the Jewish Fanny Borach (Brice). Both "Ziegfield Follies" stars had to conform to the public's conception of how they should look and act: he to "black up", she to don the traits of the "yenta", both to don a heavy, overdone "dialect".) Eventually, the overt one-dimensional portrayal of the Jewish "type" was subtly moderated, long before portrayals of such groups as blacks and Chinese.

[17]   *Jews Without Money*, by Michael Gold, contains an excellent description of Moskowitz and the restaurant.

[18]   Although the early recording industry began by issuing stereotypical ethnic portrayals, it wasn't long before the huge numbers of immigrants coming to America prodded the record companies in another direction. What they discovered was that many of these minorities would be willing to buy a gramophone and records...so long as there were recordings available representing their own group. Without hesitation, the companies issued thousands of records of numerous ethnic music traditions in transition. Most companies that issued objectionable out-group portrayals in their popular record series catalog also produced accurate and authentic in-group renditions in their ethnic catalog. Such was the nature of the business: they covered all bases.

[19]   H.W. Perlman, one of the financial backers of the fledgling "UHD&C", was also the owner of the "H.W. Perlman Piano Company" on New York's Lower East Side just a few blocks from the "UHD&C" offices on Grand and Chrystie Street. This was one of the first (and perhaps only) immigrant Jewish owned and operated instrument builder of this era. It is not surprising then, that the "UHD&C" logo is almost identical in design to the one found on Perlman pianos!

[20]   Quoted in Lynn Dion: "Klezmer Music In America: Revival and Beyond" JFEN 1986 (see bibliography). The klezmer was found in "evocative" contexts such as nostalgia motifs in popular theatre and music. The musician preferred to be referred to as musiker or, better yet, a kunstler (an artist)...not a klezmer. And rather than call their players "klezmorim", they chose a more refined "kapelye" (band) or the uptown "Orchestra". In the time before I was aware of what was on these old 78's, I turned away numerous copies of those klezmer disks billed as "Orchestra" thinking they were art music orchestral arrangements of Yiddish tunes.

[21]   Dave Tarras recalls that his biggest problem, when requested by the record company to produce several new disks, was not recording them but naming them, see notes to "Klezmer Music 1910-1942" FSS 34021.

[22]   The circumstantial similarities which bind klezmer and jazz can be seen most clearly in the music and society of black New Orleans. In both cases, it was a brass band with a strong clarinet presence which characterized the style. This instrumentation was coincidentally caused by the discarding of brass instruments by the military, which unseated an earlier string oriented tradition. Both klezmorim and the Dixieland players took the dominant music structures and scales around them and altered them to fit their own sound sense --blacks combined the "blue note" and syncopation while the Yiddish "freygish" was combined with characteristic Jewish dance rhythms-- while both were tied to a powerful vocal sense. These groups of musicians were, for the most part, at the economic mercy of white/gentile society and, as often as not, would be hired to entertain in that social strata. This was not only how both groups learned much of their out-group and art music material, but was also one route of escape from the privations of the ghetto and success in the outside world. Both groups also integrated music into certain life cycle events (the "jazz funeral", for instance). However, these mainly socioeconomic and musical coincidences fail to show true structural similarities between the "New Orleans" and "klezmer" musical forms.

[23]   Instead, the Jewish community found a more than suitable exchange with Broadway. The emergence of "Fiddler On the Roof more than any Yiddish production could, touched a very responsive part of the American Jewish community. It was both very Jewish and very American (Anatevke is Jewish; Broadway is American). Much of the music from the show has become part of the standard Jewish club date wedding ("Sunrise, Sunset",for example," has become the new "'traditional' First Waltz", etc.)

A FEW NOTES AND OBSERVATIONS ON THE THEORY AND PERFORMANCE OF KLEZMER MUSIC   BY PETE SOKOLOW

Klezmer music was originally an eastern European folk genre, heavily influenced by other existing native folk genres endemic to that area, i.e. Roumanian, Russian, Polish, Ukranian, Hungarian, Bulgarian, with a strong dose of Gypsy. What makes this music particularly individual is that it was filtered through Jewish ears and consciousness. The tradition of the *khazn* (cantor) and the *nigun* was practically inborn for the Jewish musician, a personage growing up in an ethnically segregated, religion-centered society. It must also be remembered that we are dealing, in essence, with utilitarian, dance-oriented music. Urbanity and sophistication did, indeed, begin to appear in *klezmer* music by the late 19th and early to mid-20th centuries, aided in no small measure by the development of the phonograph record, but equally by urbanization, as large numbers of "shtetl" Jews, including many *klezmorim* , moved to the cities, both in Europe and America. The resulting contact with concert music, European theater and salon music, and American ragtime/jazz and popular song, gave polish and some smoothness to the old folk style, and formed, for better or worse, a kind of second and third-generation *klezmer* music for a more modern era.

We will be looking at *klezmer* music, both earlier and later, from several aspects—dance forms, scales, harmonies, rhythmic patterns, instrument functions- emphasizing accepted performance practices, as gathered from the study of old phonograph recordings and "on-the-job training" received from older *klezmer* performers.

DANCE FORMS
The *Bulgar*, or *Freylekhs*
A lively circle dance, played at moderate to bright tempo. The rhythmic peculiarity that gives the *bulgar* its "lift" is its 8/8 meter, composed of two groups of 3 and one group of 2; 123 123 12 which adds up to eight 8ths, the equivalent in time to one 4/4 measure, or

two measures in 2/4 meter. The most basic *bulgar* (*freylekhs*) beat is:

While the drummer plays this rhythm and its variations, the piano/accordion and bass play a duple "oom-pah" beat; the resulting tension gives the Bulgar its individuality. Examples: "Shtiler Bulgar", "Varshaver Freylekhs", "Kiever", "Odesser", "Heyser" Bulgars, "A Nakht in Gan Eydn", "Bb Minor Bulgar" by Dave Tarras, "Dovid Shpil Es Nokh Amol".

The *Khosidl*
A slower dance in duple meter (2/4 or 4/4), in which the melody moves slowly enough to invite embellishment by clarinet, violin, or flute to a greater degree than allowed by the brighter Freylekh tempo. Examples: "Reb Dovid's Nigun", "Baym Rebe's Sude", "Oi Tate", "Ot Azoi". Some specialty dances, such as "Patsh Tantz" and" Broyges Tantz" , can also be included in this category.

The *Hora,* or *Zhok*
A slow Rumanian-style piece in triple meter, usually written in 3/8, whose rhythm is distinctive because of the lack of a second beat. It is played etc. 1_3 1_3   etc. The Hora also invites virtuostic ornamentation due to its slow tempo. Examples: "Kandel Hora", "Hora Mit Tzibeles", "Gasn Nigun", "Nokh A Glezel Vayn", "Firn Di Mekhutonim Aheim".

The *Terkish*
A quasi-Oriental piece in duple meter, slow-moderate in tempo, using a Habanera-like rhythm.

This form was a specialty of the great clarinetist Naftule Brandwein, and is represented here by:"Terkishe Yale V'yovo Tantz","Arabishe Tantz", "Terk in America", and "Yid In Yerushalayim", all Brandwein pieces.

The *Sher*

A set dance, similar in steps to the Virginia Reel. It is played in duple meter, usually written in 2/4, at a moderate tempo, between a *khosidl* and a *bulgar*. The drummer plays the 8/8 I rhythm at the slower tempo for the *sher*. (Example: "Russian Sher #5"), Shloimke Beckerman's "Galitsyaner Tantz",which is slower than a *bulgar*, is performed in the style of a *sher*.

The *Doina*

A rhapsodic, ametrical fantasy, often improvised, which served as a showpiece for clarinetists, violinists, mandolinists, flutists, cymbolists, accordionists, trumpeters- even xylophone and banjo doinas exist. The ensemble sustains chords while the soloist articulates. Chord changes are indicated by the soloist as the piece progresses. Usually, the *doina* is the first piece in a three-part suite that includes a *doina,* a *hora* (*zhok*), and a *bulgar* (*freylekhs*) or *khosidl* . *Klezmer* bands have also been called upon to play waltzes and mazurkas (both in 3/4 meter), polkas (2/4), tangos (4/4) European military marches (2/4 and 6/8), and popular pieces from the Yiddish theatre, often in fox-trot, waltz, tango, and even rhumba rhythms.

A Word or Two on Improvisation

It has lately become fashionable to associate *klezmer* music with jazz. Writers talk of flights of fancy, soaring emotional/creative heights, etc. Let it be stated here that we are operating in a highly proscribed, somewhat narrow musical milieu with a set vocabulary and phraseology. I would compare *klezmer* music only with the very earliest post-ragtime New Orleans/ Dixieland of the King Oliver/Original Dixieland Jazz Band stripe- an ensemble based style in which "soloing" goes on while everybody is playing, or an occasional, very short "break". The sort of chord-based improvisation endemic to later jazz is non-existent here. The *klezmer* is expected to embellish the melody in a tasteful, artistic manner; even in the case of the *doina,* the player must adhere to stringent idiomatic strictures. While it is true that a given piece may originally have been improvised, once the piece is "set", improvising is out.

MELODIC AND HARMONIC MODES

Five modes encompass the great majority of traditional *klezmer* tunes. We'll briefly examine each of them separately, beginning with the major and minor modes familiar to all students of western art music. All of the five modes presented here appear with a D as the tonic pitch, for the purpose of easier comparison of their distinctive intervallic structures. The reader should understand that all of these modes are transposable; any mode can begin on any pitch. It is the pattern of whole and half steps, not the starting note, that defines the mode.

Major

This mode needs little explanation. The half steps fall between the 3rd and 4th degree, and the 7th and 8th degree. The half step between the 7th and 8th degree is especially important in the Western music system. It provides the mode with a "leading tone", the seventh note, which has a strong melodic tendency to pull toward the upper tonic note. It also means that the dominant (V) chord will be major, since the third of this chord is the raised "leading tone". These features are crucial in defining tonality or "key".

Notice that all the primary chords: tonic (I), subdominant (IV), and dominant (V) are major in the major mode. The secondary chords ii and vi, which are minor, are used as variants for the primary chords, especially in the internal sections of a tune, where the emphasis may temporarily shift away from the primary key of the tune towards a related key.

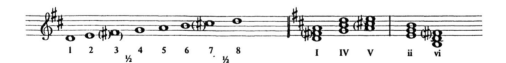

Minor

The primary difference between the major and minor modes lies in the position of the 3rd degree of the scale. In the minor, the half step falls between 2 and 3. In the upper half of the scale, some variation occurs according to one of the three forms of the minor: natural, harmonic and melodic.

The <u>natural</u> minor has no alterations away from its usual whole and half step pattern; in D, it would run as follows: D E F G A <u>Bb</u> <u>C</u> D. The <u>harmonic</u> minor, which is most common in music of the tonal period (about 1600-1900), raises the C to C#, in order to obtain that important leading tone and the major quality in the dominant chord. The <u>melodic</u> minor scale further alters the basic minor interval pattern in order to "correct" the large interval of the augmented second which occurs when the 7th degree is raised to C#; the 6th degree becomes B♮. This correction is deemed necessary in Western usage when the scale is used in a certain melodic passage. In such contexts, the augmented second might be regarded as awkward. The Harmonic minor is almost universally used in *klezmer* music.The tonic (i) and subdominant (iv) chords are minor, and the dominant, as we have already seen, is major, due to the chromatic alterations of the basic scale.

The remaining three modes are those which are specifically characteristic of Ashkenazic and other Eastern European music. A.Z.Idelsohn in his "Jewish Music in its Historical Development" has named these cantorial modes according to the first words of the prayers in which they appear: *Ahava Raba* (A"Great Love"), *Mi Sheberakh* ("He Who Blesses") and *Adonoi Molokh* ("The Lord is King"). The Idelsohn nomenclature will be used in the interest of clarity.

AHAVA RABA

This mode is commonly known as *freygish* among modern *klezmer* musicians; this probably is an adaptation of the Greek word *phrygian*, which denotes a mode with a half step between the fifth and sixth notes.[1] The *Ahava Raba* mode varies from the *phrygian* in that the third is <u>major</u> creating a wide interval of one and a half steps between the second and third. The seventh may be minor or major according to the melody. For reasons of convenience, pieces in this mode are usually written in the key of the subdominant minor (iv), because most of the notes fall into that signature. The tonic (I) chord is major and the subdominant (iv) is minor. The chord that is usually used in cadences in place of the dominant is the chord of the minor seventh, a whole step below the tonic, which is a minor triad. The *Ahava Raba* mode is referred to in Moshe Bergovski's "Old Yiddish Folk Songs" as "altered Phrygian", for reasons stated above.
A form of the *Ahava Raba* mode is in wide use in the Arab world and in non-Jewish Eastern Europe. Its Arabic counterpart travels under the name "Hijaz", with several spellings of the word.

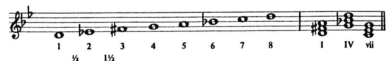

MISHEBERAKH

This mode like *Ahava Raba*, is characterized by the presence of an augmented second, this time between the 3rd and 4th degree of the scale; the 6th degree is natural and not flatted. This minor-like configuration in the first three notes and the natural 6th degree likens *Misheberakh* to the Dorian mode of medieval church usage. Misheberakh consequently is known as "altered Dorian", notably in the writings of Bergovski. Because this mode is widespread in the Ukraine [2] it is also sometimes called "Ukranian Dorian." Idelsohn notes that the mode is not very prominent in Jewish usage, except in the prayers *Misheberakh* and Ov *Horakhamim*: this would seem to imply that the use of the mode in *klezmer* and other Yiddish folk music is probably strongest in areas where non-Jewish usage reinforces it. Slobin, on the other hand, infers that the most frequent occurence of the mode is in the area of heavy Jewish population [3] that is, in Rumania, and the Ukraine.
Misheberakh presents interesting problems and possibilities of harmonization, because of its raised 4th degree. First, there can be no "normal" subdominant in the functional sense, which is built on the 4th. In the Rumanian usage, and particularly in the frequent use of this mode for the Rumanian doina, the major II chord is often used in this subdominant-like function. In later American settings, a diminished chord with a distinctive "bluesy" sonority is generated on the tonic

1. The "Greek" modes in use for medieval plainsong were themselves not really Greek. They were theoretical extrapolations of what was believed by medieval theorists to be ancient Greek usage, and bore little if any resemblance to the supposed original.   2. Idelsohn, op. cit. pg. 184-190   3. Slobin, "Tenement Songs", pg. 185.

chord, using the 1st, 3rd, and 4th degrees of the scale. (in D: using D, F, and Ab as the enharmonic equivalent of G#). Very often, the passages in the *Misheberakh* mode are harmonized only with the tonic minor chord, allowing the 4th, 6th and 7th notes to act as passing tones, or making the triad a four note minor 7th or added 6th chord. A less frequent harmonization uses the major II triad to lead the V minor (Example: "Odessa Bulgar")

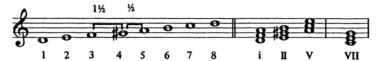

ADONOI MOLOKH

The scale of this mode follows the medieval mode know as *mixolydian* . It is essentially a major scale, except for the 7th note, which is a minor interval a whole step below the tonic. The I and IV chords are consequently major, and the V <u>should</u> be minor. For some reason, in virtually all known pieces in the *Adonoi Molokh* mode, a <u>major</u> V chord is used, and a major leading tone 7th is used below the 1 tonic (Examples: "Der Shtiler Bulgar", "Baym Rebn in Palestina")

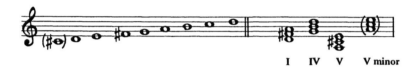

HARMONIC PHRASE STRUCTURE

Within a given *klezmer* piece, there are usually two, three, or four individual sections. Often there will be a <u>related</u> key change from section A to B, or B to C or C to D, as follows: If section A is in <u>minor</u>, section B or C may go to the RELATIVE MAJOR, the major key a minor third above the tonic (Rel. Maj. of D min.=Fmaj.) Conversely, if the piece starts in <u>major</u>, the move would be to the RELATIVE MINOR, the minor key a minor 3rd below the tonic (Rel. Min. of F maj=D min.) If section A is in *Ahava Raba*, the usual transition is to the IV (Subdom.) Minor (E *Ahava Raba*—A min., D *Ahava Raba*—G min.) A subsequent change could be to the dominant (VII Min.) (In E *Ahava Raba*—D min., in D *Ahava Raba*—C min.) Clarinetist Dave Tarras favored alternating sections in major and minor, or vice-versa, in the same key (C major-C minor, or C minor-C major).

A problem arises in the harmonization of "Eastern" (i.e. "Oriental") melodies in Western harmony. Hungarian and Gypsy musicians tended to use transitional chords, such as diminished triads and sevenths, ii and vi minor chords and secondary dominants, whereas early *klezmer* recordings show a simpler, more basic concept which allows the raised fourths, major sixths and minor sevenths to act as passing tones over a basic tonic or dominant chord.

Second generation American *klezmorim* have usually followed the Hungarian and American dance-band practice of using secondary chords and chromatic counter melodies; third generation performers generally prefer the simpler, older approach.

There are also a few common changes that do not fit the "normal" patterns. The *Ahava Raba* can go to Subdom. MAJOR,then to Subdom. Minor (Ex. E Fr.-A Maj.-A min). This "major-minor" scheme often appears in Min.-Rel. Maj.-Subdom. Maj.-Subdom. Min. (In D min: D min., F maj. G maj., G min.). An even spicier version of this progression appears in the 3/8 Hora, the "Gasn Nigun". The chords to the second half of section A of the "Gasn Nigun" read: F maj., F min., G maj., F maj. C min., D min. The minor of the relative major (F min.) and an *Ahava Raba* dominant are superimposed on this D minor melody. In all cases, careful listening will bring familiarity with basic harmonic patterns; remember that, CHORDS FOLLOW MELODY. In very few cases in this book, harmonics were substituted where the recorded performances showed errors on the part of supporting players.

SOME TIPS ON MELODIC/RHYTHMIC INTERPRETATION

Eighth notes are phrased evenly- "legit", not jazz. Dotted eighth-sixteenth rhythms likewise- long on the dotted eighth, very short on the sixteenth. The repeated eighth-note triplet figures so common in this style are usually phrased somewhere between true, even triplets and two sixteenths and an eighth. (Many older and younger players habitually phrase triplets as two sixteenths and an eighth: ♪♪♪ ♪♪♪ or ♪♪♪ ♪♪♪)

Articulation leans toward a more staccato, less legato approach; alternating tongued and slurred passages are fairly common. Trills are always very rapid. Long-held notes are often "bent"- hit on pitch, slightly flatted (NEVER raised), and brought back to pitch. There are also a number of "stock" phrases which are used to fill in on long notes or "pickups"- triplet figures, broken chords/arpeggios, glissandos, repeated notes, etc. Many of these can be found as part of the actual piece.

The standard ending for all *klezmer* pieces is a chromatic run, or glissando, into a three note 1-5-1 pattern. The player substitutes the run or glissando for the penultimate measure; the 1-5-1 may be three short notes, or short note-rest, short note-rest, long note.

Chords are I (major or minor), V major, I (major or minor.) Even the I *Zhok* uses this ending in 2/4; the *Terkish* uses it in 4/4.

In all melodic variation in klezmer style, THE MELODY COMES FIRST!! The *dreydlekh* (ornamental turns) decorate the melody, NOT VICE-VERSA. There is always the tendency for the inexperienced player to try to "throw in the kitchen sink" in trying for authenticity, or Nirvana, or whatever; this gives a flashy, shallow performance. Dig into the MUSIC and strive for ARTISTRY. Further hints will appear in the sections on instrumental function.

INSTRUMENTAL FUNCTIONS

We will group instruments in three categories: Melodic (Lead), HARMONIC SUPPORT, and Rhythm/Chord.
Category A: Melodic (Lead)
   Violin, Clarinet, Flute/Piccolo, Trumpet, Mandolin, Xylophone, Sop. Sax., Concertina.
Category B: Harmonic Support
   Alto, Tenor, Baritone Saxophones; Trombone, Mellophone, French Horn, Alto, Baritone Horn; Viola, Cello, and 2nd or 3rd of any Melodic instrument, if there are more than one in band.
Category C: Rhythm/Chord
   Piano, Accordion (incl. Bayan), Electric Keyboard, Guitar, Banjo, Bass (Upright or Electric), Tuba, Cymbalom (Tsimbl), Dulcimer, Autoharp, Drums, Percussion.

While it is common that support and rhythm instruments play melody at times, a good rule of thumb is "Form Follows Function". The higher-pitched instruments, in general, were designed to play melody, and the lower-pitched instruments to support them in the ensemble. A trombone solo is desirable and beautiful, but trombone melody/clarinet harmony sounds unnatural in a normal context; such role reversal is very effective at times for contrast, but not as the basic ensemble sound. In the case of two equals, such as clarinet and violin or alto/ tenor sax and trombone, the rule is "mix and match", i.e. alternate lead and harmony, or unison in octaves, a very effective device which obviates intonation problems common in much unison playing, especially between clarinet, violin, flute, and trumpet.

HINTS FOR ENSEMBLE PLAYING
Melodic (Lead):
The trumpet stays closest to the actual melody. Occasional finger trills, repeatedly tongued notes, and the standard neighboring-tone appogiaturas are all that is called for. Some first and second-generation players used a Ziggy Elman/Harry James tone, with wide vibrato and half-valve glissandos, to imply a Jewish inflection; the earlier players used a classical/concert band approach which suits the ensemble better. Use gimmicks sparingly, if at all. Trumpeters will have to transpose parts written in "concert" (C instrument) pitch up one tone for Bb trumpet.

The flute used in Europe was the wooden variety, which has a hollow, round, rather edge-less tone. Players relied on finger trills and tonal variation-hollow (deep) or shallow (bright). Today's metal flutes are far brighter in tone and project better, but lack the ethereal quality of wooden models. Today's flutist can trill and gliss with half-open holes. Use vibrato judiciously-not too much. Transpose most written pieces up an octave.

The violin is the original Klezmer-and Gypsy- instrument. From it comes everything. Trills, bird imitations, spiccato bowings, harmonics, glissandos up and down the fingerboard, expressive vibrato variation- the whole gamut is available to a capable violinist. Most written parts sound best transposed up an octave.Some third generation players use a style called "backup", which involves playing two or three note chords on the off beat, while another instrument carries the melody.

The clarinet has inherited the mantle of "Number One Klezmer Instrument." Clarinetists can do all sorts of tricks- "chirps", made by loosening and abruptly tightening the lower jaw; side-key trills, using the two side keys on the upper joint with the right index finger; glisses, which combine varying lip pressure and gradual finger motion, finger trills, appogiaturas, and lip vibrato. Transpose up a tone, up an octave.

The violin and clarinet are more adaptable for glissing and note-bending than are any other instruments in this category. It is quite common for melody instruments to play the same melody with different phrasing at the same time, each player playing a natural style for his/her instrument. Just follow the principle of "less is more", and use artistic discretion. By all means- trill, gliss, bend, chirp, but DON'T OVERDO IT! See musical example I for sample melodic phrasing, example II for "stock" phrase ending, example III for trill above melody, a commonly used device in which clarinet or piccolo trills a high note while others play the melody. This appears only on a repeat or Da Capo.

<u>Harmonic Support</u> instruments serve any or all of the following functions:
A. <u>Straight Harmony,</u> either ALTO (2nd trumpet, clarinet, violin; alto sax), which moves parallel to the melody at a distance of a 3rd or 4th below (Ex. IV), or TENOR (3rd trumpet, clarinet, violin; alto or tenor sax, trombone, viola, cello), which moves at a 6th or 5th below (Ex. IV B). The player thinks a 3rd/4th above while playing in a lower octave.
B. <u>Counter-Melody,</u> a simple, slow-moving counterpoint to the melody, which can be played by one instrument, or by two more in unison. (Ex.V)
C. <u>Quasi-Bass</u>, the basic trombone function, which can also be played effectively by tenor or baritone sax, or baritone horn. This comprises a rhythmic, punchy counter-melody which approximates a bass line and 8/8 rhythm (Ex. VI).

The tenor harmony is often played by a lead instrument <u>above</u> the melody. When doing this, the harmony player <u>must</u> play at a volume level <u>below</u> that of the melody player to achieve the correct blend and to avoid overshadowing the lead line.

<u>Chord-Rhythm Instruments</u>
These are the foundation of the *klezmer* band. They play the "oom-pahs," bass lines, and percussive fundamentals; some can solo effectively in a melodic and counter-melodic sense. The piano and accordion (bayan) were added somewhat later in *klezmer* history, but soon became virtually indispensable; the same can be said of the drum set. Electric keyboards, guitar, and banjo, all added recently, are found in many klezmer groups, and can be used to good advantage.
The <u>piano</u> is basically used for "oom-pahs", in duple or triple meters. The pianist can vary the basic beat with the use of sustained "thumb-notes", or with chorded octaves (Ex. VII, VII A, VII B). Chords for accompaniment sound best in close-voiced inversions in the lower-middle range; use a crisp, staccato attack and not too much pedal. In the bass, use low single notes and octaves crisply. One can also create bass-line/right hand movement in tenths, with octaves giving a full effect. (Ex. VIII)
The <u>accordion</u> can be very flexible, due to its built in left hand "oom-pah". The right hand is free to sustain chords or punctuate rhythmically (Ex. IX, IX A). The right hand can also play alto or tenor harmony, simple or complex counter-melodies, or play lead, in trumpet-like style or in 3rds or 6ths.
The <u>electric keyboard</u> player should aim for as "acoustic" a sound as possible. The left hand is a bass player, the right a piano or accordion. Generally a split bass is desired, turned <u>off</u> in the presence of a bass player. No vibratos, please, and keep the volume at a nice blend. The use of synthesized sounds (strings, brass, reeds, etc.) usually "blankets" a band and should be used very sparingly, if at all.
The <u>bass</u> is a real plus. The acoustic string bass can be bowed or plucked- some players use the bow to great effect, even on fast *bulgars* ! Arco is marvellous behind a *doina.*. In the absence of a string bass, an electric ("Fender" or "bass guitar") may be used, provided that a deep, acoustic-like tone is employed. The <u>tuba,</u> of course, can do much of what the plucked/bowed bass does, given enough *koykekh* (strength) in the player. Bass lines are always in 2, not 8/8, for *bulgars, shers,* etc. Lines can "walk" (Ex. X).
The <u>guitar</u> and <u>banjo</u> can be used for chordal accompaniment, in 2 or 8/8, or for single-string melody or counter-melody. The author of this book has demonstrated the effectiveness of the banjo for fast and slow accompaniment in his recordings with "Kapelye", and has recently recorded a single-string *doina*. (See Ex. XI, XI A for accompaniment). A melodic alternative is the <u>mandolin</u>, once enormously popular in Europe. This instrument lends a distinctive solo voice, utilizing the rapid up-and-down stroke quasi-tremolo; it can be used as a "double" by guitarist, banjoist, or violinist. Clarinetist Andy Statman is a virtuoso mandolinist as well.

And now, we come to the <u>drums</u>. Fine *klezmer* drumming can really be called an art, for it requires doing a lot with a little. The basics are: snare drum, cymbal, bass drum, and WOODBLOCK! Hi-hat cymbals and tom toms are recent additions and are hardly used in this style. The drummer uses a "press-roll" style on the snare drum most of the time, in seemingly endless 8/8 and 2/4 variations, with judicious use of cymbals. The woodblock is used in the middle of a *bulgar* or *sher-* repeat of 2nd or 3rd section - for variety. See Ex. XII A, B, C, D, E, F for basic drum patterns. Other percussion used in *klezmer* music include sleighbells, shaken in 8th note patterns, and tambourine, usually hit and shaken in 8/8 or 2/4 patterns. (Ex. XII G, H)

A few final observations, if I may. Above all, *klezmer* music is DANCE MUSIC. Tempos and volume should be MODERATE. Time should be rock-steady (no rushing), and phrasing should be crisp and rhythmic. Respect the integrity of style and melody-too many *dreydlekh* spoil the *tsholnt*. (stew). A band is a TEAM- each player pulls his/her weight, none trying to out-do the other. Klezmer is an ensemble form, and egotism/exhibitionism tend to throw the music out of balance. The result should be a musically valid, relaxed performance, with more than a dollop of <u>humor</u>, for the essence of playing this kind of "earthy" music is that it should be FUN, for listener and performer alike.

MUSIC EXAMPLES

28

The 33 tunes presented here are taken from performances recorded in the years 1912-1939. A cassette entitled "The Compleat Klezmer" (SC-02) containing excerpts of the original recordings is available from "Global Village Music" (see discography for address). The transcriptions are standardized renderings of these original recordings, so we recommend use of the cassette in conjunction with the written music to deepen the understanding of ornamentation, phrasing, variations, etc.

Sections of tunes will be indicated by a " " around the letter while the key letter will not.

Kapelye, 1985
Lauren Brody, accordion; Michael Alpert, fiddle; Ken Maltz, clarinet, Eric Berman, tuba, Henry Sapoznik, banjo.

Bb MINOR BULGAR

as played by DAVE TARRAS   (♩=115-120)

This Tarras composition is written in his beloved key, concert Bb minor which brings out the woody middle and lower registers of the Bb clarinet, one of Tarras' many trademarks. The melody, of course, is elegant and totally balanced, classically harmonized---evidence of Tarras' attention to the minute detail of tune construction. The "B" section is in the relative major, Db, and the "C" goes back to Bb minor.

Dave Tarras in a typically classic mid 1940's pose (Photo
courtesy Dave Tarras)

DOVID, SHPIL ES NOKH A MOL

(PLAY IT AGAIN, DAVE)

as played by DAVE TARRAS 1939 (♩=105-110)

Originally part of a larger Decca session under the baton of violinist and bandleader Al Glaser (1898-1982) and his "Bukovina Kapelle", this bulgar represents classic Tarras. It has been raised from C major, the original key, to F major, (the standard on-the-job performance key) for the consideration of wind players. The essentially Rumanian cast of the melody is typically "Dave" (he was born in the Ukraine, just next door to Rumania). Some exercise book" sections (like the scales in the "B" part) are frequently found in Tarras performances. The relative minor in C, leading back to major on the repeat of "A".

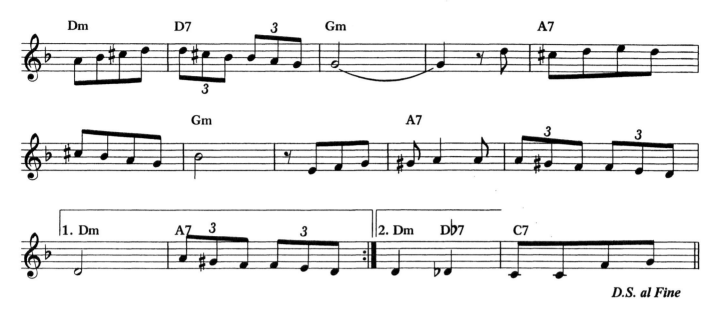

Dave Tarras at age 9 in Ternovka, Ukraine
1907 (Photo courtesy of Dave Tarras).

DER HEYSER BULGAR

(THE HOT BULGAR)

NAFTULE BRANDWEIN ORCHESTRA 1923 (♩=115-120)

This piece uses all the harmonics of *Ahava Raba*—I major, IV minor and VII minor. The 16th notes at the end of the "A" are all slurred except for the first note;while in the "C" section, be sure to bend the long held C note and observe the stop time. "Der Heyser" was introduced to vaudeville audiences by Brandwein soloing with Joseph Cherniavsky's Yiddish American Jazz Band in 1924. It was Tarras, however who was to record it under the name "Khasene Nigunim" with Cherniavsky after he replaced Brandwein in 1925. This most complete composition is, in so many words, a classic.

KIEVER BULGAR

(BULGAR FROM KIEV)

HARRY KANDEL'S ORCHESTRA 1921 (♩ =105-110)
This tune contains some Hasidic overtones in the "A" section, and a "shout chorus" to boot . The harmony in the "B" section contains some fascinating *Misheberakh*, relative major F minor-G major cadences. The "C" section is a rather stock relative major.

KISHINIEVER BULGAR

(BULGAR FROM KISHINIEV)

ABE SCHWARTZ'S ORCHESTRA 1917   (♩=105-110)
This tune is almost completely in major except for the *Adonoi Molokh* in the "B" section. It has a
Rumanian/Russian flavor and a simplicity of melody which lends itself well to embellishment.

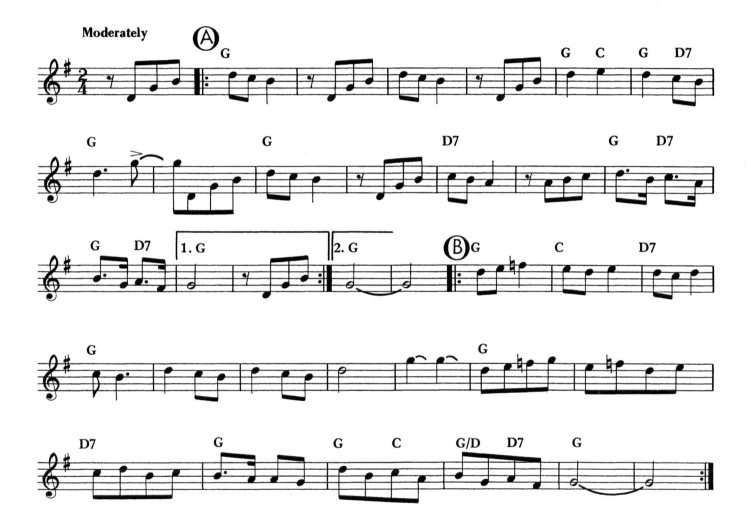

A NAKHT IN GAN EYDN

(A NIGHT IN THE GARDEN OF EDEN)

HARRY KANDEL'S ORCHESTRA 1926 (♩=110-115)
A melody with a strong Hasidic cast to it. Note the minor-major phrase repeats in the "A" section coupled with a nice harmonic motion in the "B". Note the suprise D major chord to F which appears in bars 9 and 10 of the "C". The original recording abounds in chirps and trills over the melody. Kandel composed and recorded this tune in 1924 on an acoustic Brunswick and waxed it again 2 years later on an improved Victor electrical disc.

ODESSA BULGARISH

(BULGAR FROM ODESSA)

ABE SCHWARTZ ORCHESTRA 1919   (♩=100-110)
Here is a lively bulgar in D *Misheberakh*. The harmonization set down here follows the Schwartz arrangement, especially in the "B" section where the minor dominant, A minor, is used. This tune, published in 1921, is an example of one of the very few *klezmer* melodies issued by the Hebrew Publishing Company.

D.S. al Fine

DER SHTILER BULGAR

(THE QUIET BULGAR)

HARRY KANDEL'S ORCHESTRA 1917 (♩=100)

The old standard which became, through the good offices of one Ziggy Elman (nee Harry Finkelman), a swing standard called "And the Angels Sing". Straight C major throughout the "A" section, with plenty of room for trills, etc. The *Adonoi Molokh* is introduced in the "B" section with a suprise two measures in C minor; the "C" section is in relative minor and the use of the woodblock is most effective there.

D.C. al Fine

VARSHAVER FREYLEKHS

(FREYLAKHS FROM WARSAW)

ABE SCHWARTZ ORCHESTRA 1920 (♩=115-120)

A Gypsy-ish melody mixing minor and *Misheberakh* with a "C" section in major. The "B" section sounds a little like a minor version of that used in "Shtiler Bulgar". As Schwartz played it, there is a brighter tempo than usual on this one.

SIRBA

as played by DAVE TARRAS   (♩ =110-115)

This classic, a real favorite of Tarras disciples, is nicknamed "The Bumblebee", because of its rapidly moving melodic line. A favorite Tarras device appears in the "B" section—Dave was always fond of putting a major section in a minor piece, and vice versa, in the same key. Here, the major appears in a basically minor composition (where Dave's "Exercise Book" abounds). The "Sirba" has been transcribed in D minor, instead of the original Bb minor, to facilitate its execution by non-clarinetists, who may find Tarras' preferred key a bit of an obstacle course.

FIRN DI MEKHUTONIM AHEYM

(ESCORTING THE PARENTS OF THE BRIDE AND BRIDEGROOM)

NAFTULE BRANDWEIN 1923 (♩=60)

One of the finest of all compositions in the *klezmer* genre, this may be the most Tarras-like of all Brandwein's pieces. The melody is flowing, yet gutsy; the performance is commanding—simple, yet virtuostic. Beginning in D *Ahava Raba* it goes to the IV minor in the "B" section. The harmonization penned by Abe Schwartz of the long held notes in the "C" section is interesting: G minor, Bb major, Eb major, C minor. All are related yet unusual in juxtaposition. The endings of all the sections are identical, but this sounds natural and not at all repetitive.

Slow Hora

D.C. Last time al ⊕

Naftule Brandwein (seated center) with Azriel Brandwein
(left with trumpet), ? Shuster (right, with trumpet),
? Shpielman (upper right with trombone) others unknown.
ca. 1920

BAYM REBIN IN PALESTINA

(AT THE RABBI IN PALESTINE)

BRODER KAPELLE 1929   (♩=70)

This piece is in the *Adonoi Molokh* mode and also lends itself to trills, appogiatures, etc. The Broder Kapelle, led by clarinetist Itzikl Kramtweiss, was a popular band on the Philadelphia *klezmer* scene. Kramtweiss had a rougher sound than that of either Brandwein or Tarras, but was exciting nonetheless. Moshe Beregovski, and fellow Soviet Yiddish folklorist Itzik Fefer, collected and published a similar tune in their "Yidishe Folkslider" (Kiev, 1938).

D.C.

DER GASN NIGUN

THE STREET TUNE

KANDEL'S ORCHESTRA 1923 (♩=60)

A beautifully evocative, harmonically interesting piece whose "A" section wanders from D minor to the relative F major through F minor, G major, and back to D minor. The "B" section is a classic *Misheberakh*, in which a D minor chord suffices for the entire section. This piece has remained one of two most popular *zhok* sections in standard doina suites.

HORA MIT TSIBELES

(HORA AND ONIONS)

NAFTULE BRANDWEIN'S ORCHESTRA 1925 (♩ =75)

This piece starts out in a Greek style, goes Jewish in the "B" and "C" parts, and then finishes in Greek / Rumanian in the "D" (which may explain why this recording was simultaneously released in both the Jewish and Rumanian catalogs.) Notice the mixture of major, minor and *Ahava Raba* chord and scale patterns and the unusual rhythym at the "D".

KANDEL'S HORA

HARRY KANDEL'S ORCHESTRA 1918 (♩=60)
A classic *Ahava Raba* , using the form ABCB ("D" is the same as "B") Though section "C" is clearly in the key of G minor, the piece ends in the *Ahava Raba* mode.

A "modern" *kapelye* (sans yarmulkes) from the shtetl of Ostrovke in the Polish province of Rodomer, ca. 1905. (Photo courtesy of YIVO Institute)

NOKH A GLEZL VAYN

(ANOTHER GLASS OF WINE)

as played by DAVE TARRAS 1929 (♩. =70-75)

A hora, classically smooth and elegant, which stands out in sharp contrast to the jagged, adventurous Brandwein style. Tarras glides and swoops where Brandwein rips and tears. The piece is a mixture of straight minor and minor *Misheberakh* , and relies on elegance and balance rather than excitement and suprise. Clarinetists and violinists should play this tune in its written range.

Slow mod. Hora

Joe Helfenbein (left) former drummer in Joseph Cherniavsky's
Yiddish-American Jazz Band (1925) with Henry Sapoznik
1980 (Photo Ricki Rosen)

MOLDAVIAN HORA

V.BELUFA 1913

(♩ =70-75)

This transcription was adapted from a European recording which has an almost pastoral feeling to it. The "B" section holds many suprises—G *Ahava Raba* , G and C major, and G *Ahava Raba* again leading into A which acts as the dominant for the "A" section. Lots of trills and chirps here.

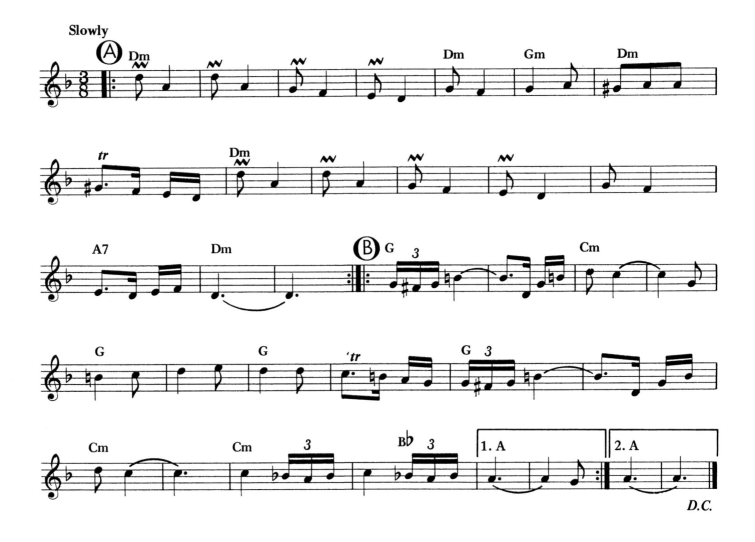

D.C.

ARABER TANTZ

(ARABIC DANCE)

NAFTULE BRANDWEIN ORCHESTRA 1926 (♩ =125)
A very Oriental-Sephardic melody, in a style recently revived by Hasidic bands as the aforementioned "debka". The lead in phrase to "C" and the descending 16ths, are typical of Brandwein's playing. The melody is rather simple and is treated as such by Brandwein on the recording.

TERK IN AMERIKA

(THE TERK IN AMERICA)

NAFTULE BRANDWEIN ORCHESTRA 1924 (♩=125)
This piece uses a popular Greek-Turkish melody called "Ulan, Ulan" or "Uskudar" coupled with Brandwein's embellishments for sections "A" and "B". Brandwein interprets the rhythm very freely in the "C" section. Try your luck on the 16ths near the end of "C" (and hope to come out on the first beat of the next bar when you should...)

Sid Beckerman, clarinet; Stu Brotman, bass at
"KlezKamp" 1985. (Photo by Judith Helfand)

TERKISHE YALE V'YOVE TANTZ

NAFTULE BRANDWINE ORCHESTRA 1923   (♩=120. ♩ not ♪, is basic beat)

A tribute to the daring clarinet virtuosity of the composer. Minor-major-minor-IV minor, *Ahava Raba* Rapid triplets in "C", dotted rhythms typical of Brandwein's terkish style. Tempo is on the bright side, so tongue and fingers really have to move. Though it is clear that Brandwein himself named this tune (more than 20% of his titles have his name in them) it is not clear why he chose the name of a Festival prayer, unless the melody of the tune is based on the shteyger of the "Yale V'Yove".

Mod. Terkish

Pete Sokolow (keyboard) and Henry Sapoznik on the set of the
1982 film "The Chosen". (Photos by Ken Maltz)

DER YID IN YERUSHOLAYIM

(THE JEW IN JERUSALEM)

NAFTULE BRANDWEIN'S ORCHESTRA 1924 (♩ =125)

Another "Nifty" masterpiece, and extremely tricky to play. The introduction of Bb (major third below, relative major of IV G minor) in the ""C" part is rounded out by the *Ahava Raba* dominant (C minor), leading back to "D" in a beautifully balanced section.

D.C.

BAYM REBIN'S SUDE

(AT THE RABBI'S TABLE)

ABE SCHWARTZ ORCHESTRA 1917 (♩=70-75)
A *Khosidl* in E *Ahava Raba*. The "B" section was also used by Joseph Cherniavsky in his
"Wedding Scenes", and more recently in hasidic bands in Arabic style called debka. On the original
Abe Schwartz recording, Brandwein, as usual, trills, glisses and chirps along.

FREYT AYKH YIDELEKH

(GET HAPPY, JEWS)

NAFTULE BRANDWEIN ORCHESTRA (♩ =75-80)

A lovely Brandwein piece, in which he consistantly substitutes the *Ahava Raba* dominant,
C minor for the more normal minor dominant, A7. The "B" section is in relative major.
The "C" section seems to indicate F minor in the first 2 bars, (the original recording,
however, has a D minor accompaniment.)

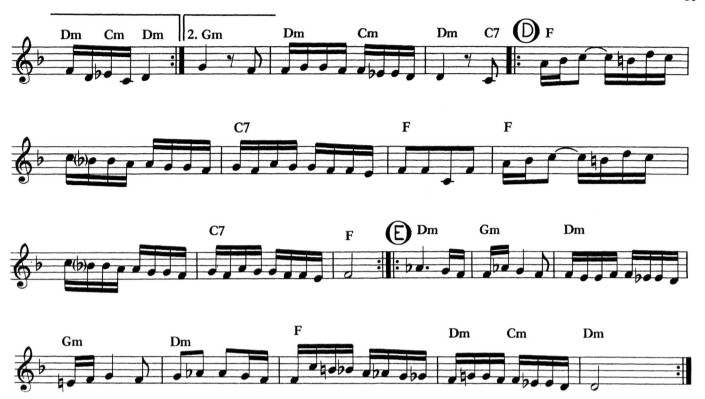

Alter Goizman Kapelye Chudnov, Volhynia,
Poland c. 1905 (Photo courtesy Louis Grupp)

OT AZOI

(THAT'S THE WAY)

SHLOIMKE BECKERMAN (ABE SCHWARTZ ORCHESTRA) 1923   (♩ =90-95)
A bright *khosidl* by another talented clarinetist, Shloimke Beckerman (1889- 1974). Similar in melodic phrases to "Baym Rebn's Sude, vocal breaks as in "Oi Tate"; the rhythm stops and the ensemble sings "ot azoi...git azoi"(it's good that way).

OI, TATE

(OH, DADDY)

LT. JOSEPH FRANKEL'S OCHESTRA 1919   (♩=85-90)

A classic *Khosidl* with ample "chirps" and trills over the melody on the original recording. Observe the vocal break in "D"--the tune comes to a complete stop followed by an "Oi, Tate". This is totally in D *Ahava Raba*.

TANTZ, TANTZ, YIDELEKH

(DANCE, DANCE JEWS)

ABE SCHWARTZ ORCHESTRA 1917   ($\quad$ = 85-90)

The quintessential "Jewish melody" before the advent of "Hava Nagila" (see Introduction, "Ma Yofus"). The piece clearly demonstrates the relation of the I major and the IV minor in *Ahava Raba* harmony and the "B" section uses the relative major. Much "chirping" evident in the original recording (most probably by Brandwein) and sleigh bells in the "B" section.

BROYGES TANTZ

(DANCE OF ANGER AND RECONCILLIATION)

HARRY KANDEL'S ORCHESTRA 1921   (♩=90-95)

A very simple folk melody in moderate *khosidl* tempo. Much trilling, "laughing" at phrase endings, chirps, etc. (The Kandel recording also has the distinction of being the only known *klezmer* disk using a steam calliope in the rhythm section!) Originally, this was a dance between the two *mekhutenistes* (mothers of the bride and groom) and was employed as a ritual expunging of the friction felt between new in-laws. The first section, played slowly, evoked the suspicion and anger of the mothers, while the second section, played at a brighter tempo represented the harmonious joining of the families (either a bulgar is played in the fast section, or the broyges tantz played as a bulgar.) In recent years a *broyges tantz* has been reinserted into the contemporary Hasidic scene as the "Tkhies Hameysim" dance though the theme is no longer fueding mother-in-laws but fighting, accidental death and resurrection between two Hasidim.This melody was also used in the lovesong "Bistu Mit Mir Broyges" published in "60 Folkslider" by Menakhem Kipnis (Warsaw, 1918).

GALITZYANER TANTZ

(A DANCE FROM GALICIA)

SHLOIMKE BECKERMAN (ABE SCHWARTZ ORCHESTRA) 1923   (♩=100-105)

A virtuoso piece that requires enormous breath control, or circular breathing. Beckerman's recording sounds as if he takes the entire "A" section on one breath, doing the same on the repeat. The harmony is fascinating: it is essentially C *Ahava Raba* in the "A" section and C minor in the "B" and "C", though it doesn't stay in any one place long enough to give a stable harmonic feel. The original is in concert A and has been transposed to concert C to facilitate smoothness of performance. Beckerman's "laugh" (bar 3 of "B" on the repeat) — is a Ted Lewis device commonly used by early jazz players—and is done by loosening the lower jaw rapidly on descending notes. This piece demonstrates the consummate skill of a performer who was too little known and recorded during his long career.

PATSH TANTZ

(HAND CLAPPING DANCE)

HARRY KANDEL ORCHESTRA 1921 (♩ =100-105)
The recording from which this transcription comes is much faster than the more recent "folk dance" version. This piece is phrased like a sher without much ornamentation. Observe the markings in the "B" section: Rhythm out 1st measure, play "clapping", rhythm 2nd measure. The "C" section is very polka-like while the "D" is a variation on "B".

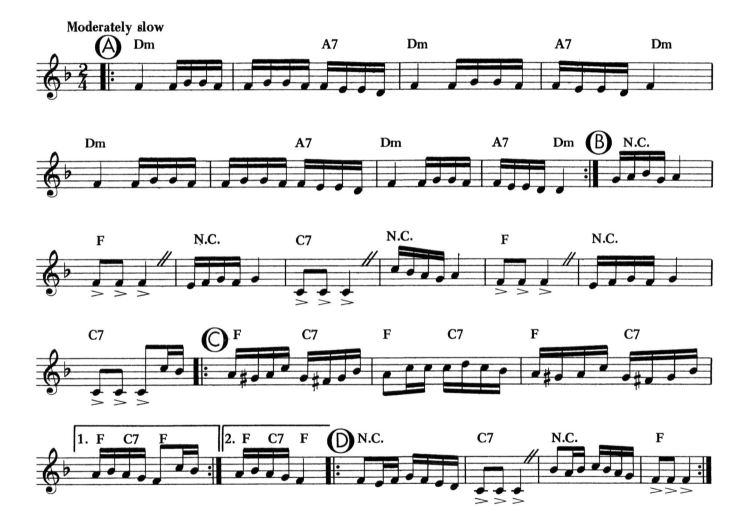

RUSSIAN SHER #5

ABE SCHWARTZ ORCHESTRA 1923 (♩=95-100)

The *sher* , literally the "scissors", is one of the most quintessentially Yiddish dances (though Beregovski notes the overwhelming absence of any mention of it in memoirs or ethnographic papers) which is structurally similar to the American square dance. This is an excerpted form of a long suite, or medley; it was, and is, usual to play *shers* in medleys. This particular grouping starts off similarly to some Hasidic marches. The "C" section, after the "shout chorus", reads like a polka. The constant 16th note motion leaves little room for interpretation.

Hankus Netsky, sax; Joel Rubin, clarinet; Marc Smason,
trombone; Henry Sapoznik, tenor banjo at "KlezKamp" 1985.
(Photo by Judith Helfand)

SHVER UN SHVIGER

(FATHER-IN-LAW MOTHER-IN-LAW)

ABE SCHWARTZ ORCHESTRA 1920   (♩=85-90)
This is a rather Hasidic sounding melody which is played quite slowly. The Hasidic "shout chorus"
before the "B" section leads into the relative major, and back to the minor at the "C" using an
Ahava Raba dominant. Brandwein, the clarinetist on the orginal recording, "chirps" the first two
quarter notes. In 1921, "SHVER UN SHVIGER..." was issued for Schwartz by the Yiddish
music publisher S. Schenker and sons.

RUMANIAN DOINA

NAFTULE BRANDWEIN 1923 (Ad lib no tempo)

The opening phrase of this piece has been used by countless first and second generation American *klezmorim* to start their doinas, but there the resemblance ends. Brandwein's exceedingly free and adventurous phrasings are hard to duplicate--they are approximated here, as in his other pieces. The primary interest in this doina lies in the chord structure of the "B" section. The modified Dorian scale of the *Misheberakh* with its raised 4th and major 6th, implies not only a G major subdominant but also a powerful secondary chord—that of the second degree of the scale, in this case, E. The raised 4th in the scale makes the E chord major ; this is often found in Rumanian gypsy pieces and bulgars. The spice comes in the transition to G minor, a natural lead-in back to D minor.

"Der Blinder Musikant" (The Blind Musician)
Polish Postcard ca. 1907 (courtesy of the YIVO
Institute) NP.

DOINA

DAVE TARRAS 1929   (Ad lib--no tempo)

This doina bears all of the hallmarks of Tarras' style. It is in the minor freygish mode, with sparse chord changes--almost all in C minor, with only momentary moves to F minor and F major. It is quite violin-like in most melodic turns, becoming more "clarinetistic" at the F major 6/4 bar. The phrasing is basically very legato, almost vocal in rubato, and grace notes are "suggested" rather than hit.

SELECTED DISCOGRAPHY AND BIBLIOGRAPHY

RECORDINGS:

FIRST GENERATION: These are recordings made by old world born and trained musicians who came to America in the first decades of the 20th century.

REISSUES: These albums represent anthologies of the earliest recorded klezmer music in both the United States and Europe. In most cases, these performances were recorded not long after the player's arrival in America.

"Klezmer Music 1910-1942"
"Klezmer Music 1910-1926"
"Jakie Jazz'em Up 1912-1926"
"The Compleat Klezmer" companion to the book of the same name
"Klezmer Pioneers"
"Nafule Brandwein"

The following recordings represent recordings made by emigre musicians in America years after their arrival. Many more albums were recorded by Tarras all of which, except these, are out of print and difficult to find.
Dave Tarras "Frailach Music"
Dave Tarras   "Master of the Jewish Clarinet"
Leon Schwartz "Klezmer Violinist"

SECOND GENERATION: These are albums recorded by American born musicians who learned their music in the 1920's-1950's from the previous group of European born klezmorim.

Sid Beckerman, Howie Leess "Klezmer Plus"
Ray Musiker   "The New York Klezmer Ensemble"
Ray Musiker   "Tzena, Tzena"
Sam Musiker   "Bulgars Fast, Medium and Slow"
Pete Sokolow "The Original Klezmer Jazz Band"
Pete Sokolow "Kosher Kitschin'"

THIRD GENERATION: These recordings represent those musicians who began playing and recording klezmer music in the 1970's after exposure to older klezmorim and/or 78 rpm's.

Feidman, Giora

"Klassic Klezmer"
"Magic of the Klezmer"
"Dance of Joy"
"Gershwin & the Klezmer
"Viva El Klezmer"
"The Singing Clarinet"
"Soul Chai
"Silence and Beyond"

KAPELYE
"Future and Past"
"Levine and His Flying Machine"
"Chicken"

KLEZMER CONSERVATORY BAND
"Yiddishe Renaissance"
"Klez"
"A Touch of Klez"
"Oy, Chanukah"

THE KLEZMORIM
"East Side Wedding"
"Streets of Gold"
"Metropolis"

ANDY STATMAN
"Andy Statman Klezmer Orchestra"
"Klezmer Suite"
"Songs of Our Fathers"
"Songs of The Mystics"

FOURTH GENERATION: These are recordings made by groups who began playing after exposure to reissues and/or recordings/concerts by Third generation musicians.

ITZHAK PERLMAN
"In the Fiddler's House"
"Live in the Fiddler's House"

KLEZMER CONSERVATORY BAND
"Klez"
"A Jumpin' Night in the Garden of Eden"
"Yiddishe Renaissance"
"A Touch of Klez"
"Dancing in the Aisles"

The KLEZMATICS
"Rhythm and Jews"
"Jews With Horns"
"Possessed"

THE YALE KLEZMER BAND
"Another Glass of Wine"

SHEET MUSIC

Feidman, Giora	"From the Repertoire of Giora Feidman"
Feidman, Giora	"Klassic Klezmer"
Feidman, Giora	"Magic of the Klezmer"
Feidman, Giora	"The Dance of Joy"
Feidman, Giora	"The Klezmer Wedding Book"
Feidman, Giora	"Easy Klezmer"
Fishman, Jay	"Mazel Tov Klezmer Style"
Kushner, Sy	"The Klezmer Fake Book" Vols. 1 & 2
Milstein, Seymour	"Klezmerantics"
Neshomo Orchestra	"Klezmer Wedding Band Folio"
Neshomo Orchestra	"Jewish Wedding Music for String Quartet"
Pasternak, Velvel	"The Jewish Play-Along"
Richmond, Ken	"Klezmer Band Folio" C & Bb editions
Rosenberg, Marvin	"Dance Klezmer Style"
Sapoznik, Henry	"Klezmer Plus"
Sokolow, Peter	"Klezmer Arranging & Orchestration"
Sokolow, Peter	"Klezmer Piano"
Sapoznik, Henry	"Klezmer Plus Piano & Keyboard Guide"
Springer, Matt	"Jewish Folksong Suite for String Quartet"